FINDING YOUR F.L.O.W.

FINDING YOUR F.L.O.W.

Answering the Writer's Call Through
Faith, Love, Obedience, and Worship

DEBORAH A. GASTON

Cincinnati, OH

Copyright © 2020 by Deborah A. Gaston

All rights reserved. No part of this book may be reproduced in any form, including written, electronic, recording, or photocopying, without written permission of the author. The exception would be in the case of brief quotations embodied in the critical articles or reviews and pages where permission is specifically granted by the author.

Although every precaution has been taken to verify the accuracy of the information contained herein, the author and publisher assume no responsibility for errors or omissions. No liability is assumed for damages that may result from the use of information contained within.

Unless otherwise indicated, Bible quotations are taken from The Holy Bible, New King James Version of the Bible. Copyright © 1982 by Thomas Nelson, Inc. Used by permission. All rights reserved.

Scriptures indicated AMP, NLT, NASB, RSV, MSG, TPT, The Mirror, The Voice are from:
The Amplified Bible Copyright © 1954, 1958, 1962, 1964, 1987 by
Zondervan Bible Publishers and the Lockman Foundation
The Holy Bible, New Living Translation, Copyright©1996, 2004 by Tyndale Charity Trust
The Holy Bible, New American Standard Bible Copyright © 1960, 1962, 1963, 1968, 1971, 1972, 1973, 1975, 1977, 1995 by The Lockman Foundation
Revised Standard Version of the Bible, copyright © 1946, 1952, and 1971 the Division of Christian Education of the National Council of the Churches of Christ in the United States of America Used by permission. All rights reserved.
The Message. Copyright © 1993, 1994, 1995, 1996, 2000 2001, 2002. Used by permission of NavPress Publishing Group
The Passion Translation®. Copyright © 2017 by BroadStreet Publishing® Group, LLC. Used by permission. All rights reserved. thePassionTranslation.com
The MIRROR. Copyright © 2012. Used by permission of The Author
The Voice Bible, Copyright © 2012 Thomas Nelson, Inc. The Voice™ Translation © 2012 Ecclesia Bible Society All rights reserved.

Photographer: Shawndale Thomas www.shawndale.com

Cover Design: Alicia Redmond www.aliciaredmond.com/bookcoversmatter

Deborah A. Gaston
6688 Twinridge Lane
Cincinnati, OH 45224
www.deborahgaston.com

IBSN (Paperback): 978-1-7344677-0-3

E-Book: 978-1-7344677-3-4

*For all lovers of words and of The Word
And all called to change the world through writing*

Contents

Acknowledgments   xi
Preface   xiii
A Writer's Prayer   xv

Introduction

A Worshiper's Writing Journey   1

Writing as Worship

Reflection: A Call to Worship   9
The Worship-Writing Connection   12
Worship Re-imagined   14
Remember Who You Are   16
Create a Writing Worship Practice through Journaling   18

Faith

Reflection: On Being a Kingdom Writer   25
An Act of Faith, An Act of Worship   28
Faith: A Prerequisite for Writing   30
The Fear Factor   32
Faith and Vulnerability   35
Faith and Freedom   37

In Search of Inspiration   39

Love

Reflection: Why I Write   45
Expressions of Love   48
For Love of Purpose   50
The Place of Passion   52
Nourished and Empowered by Love   55
Writer, Know Thyself   56

Obedience

Reflection: A Simple Response   61
Obedience: Faith's Fruit   64
Settle It and Write   65
Yes to the Lord, Yes to the Work   66
Commitment, Not Convenience   68
A Goal and a Plan   70
Finding Your Voice   73

Worship

Reflection: The Glory's in the Finish   79
The Worshipful Work of Writing   82
The Worship of Our Words   86
Worth It All   89
Putting It All Together   91

   Afterthoughts   93

   Endnotes   95

   Bibliography   97

The only book that should ever be written is one that flows up from the heart, forced out by the inward pressure. When such a work has gestated within a man it is almost certain that it will be written.

A.W. Tozer *The Pursuit of Man*

Acknowledgments

There are many hidden faces behind the writing, editing and publication of a book. Whether through words of encouragement and prayer, or by way of giving feedback and suggestions, proofreading, editing, designing and re-designing covers, it really does take a village. *Finding Your F.L.O.W.* is a reality because of my village.

First to my parents, William and Phyllis Gaston—Even now I sense you cheering me on. Dad, I am grateful for the days that I sat with you in your big green chair and you told me incredible stories. Mom, I am grateful for the nights we snuggled in bed and you read to me. You both gave me a love for words and books. Most importantly, you taught me to love *The Word*. Maybe the seed—this idea of writing as worship—began much earlier in my life than I realized as you taught me to love God, cultivate the gifts He'd given me and use them to honor Him and bless others. I am so grateful to you for sparking my curiosity, nurturing my imagination and encouraging my creativity.

To the wonderful women and men who gathered with me monthly through the F.L.O.W. Writers Connect group—I put out the call and you responded overwhelmingly to come together, to write, to share and to encourage one another. You may never know the depth of gratitude I feel for each of you. Each month you showed up and encouraged me as I endeavored to encourage you. You said, "Deborah, I believe you can do this!" whenever I shared what I believed God was speaking to me concerning F.L.O.W. You are some of the most gifted writers I know, and this book is now complete because you encouraged me to share this perspective with other worshipers who write. You are my writing tribe and I love each you!

From the time we met, Apostle John W. Stevenson, you have been a source of inspiration and encouragement to me. You have always seen the potential in me to do so much more than I dreamed. You have been that force pushing me to become all that God created me to be, and one on whom I can depend to speak truth to me in love. You challenged me in one simple conversation many years ago to press into God for a deeper revelation of worship. And that challenge spawned this book. I am grateful for your spiritual guidance as my pastor and for your friendship.

To my lifelong brother-friend, Pastor Robert W. Harper, you are a constant in my life. Thank you for being the one I can always bounce ideas off. You help me bring order to this sometimes chaotic writer's mind, and to bring logic to that which sounds illogical. I appreciate photo shoots in the park on crispy autumn days followed by pizza and impromptu Bible studies. You have always made me feel safe to be my authentic self, even when that self is a little crazed or a bit unhinged. Most of all, I am grateful that you have loved me unconditionally for over 60 years.

Heavenly Father, thank You! Thank You for inviting me into this most extraordinary journey in You. Thank You for entrusting me with this message and birthing something in me that truly is "exceeding abundantly above" all I could imagine. It is all by Your grace! This book is my offering of worship to You. May You be glorified in and through each word!!

Preface

> *Creativity requires faith. Faith requires that we relinquish control.*
> Julia Cameron *The Artist's Way*

The book you are now reading is the result of a simple response to the voice of God. I wish I could say it is the book I always dreamed of writing. I can't. Of all the ideas for books, of all the notes on scraps of paper, of all the words, songs, characters that run rampant through my overly-active imagination, of all the rough drafts pleading for completion, of all the journals teeming with topics and ideas to be explored, a book about writing is not among them.

But God dropped the seed for this book in my worshiper-writer's womb, and it began to take on a life of its own. It began to grow in me, allowing me to feel its steady, yet faint heartbeat. A kick now and then. A shift in position at unexpected moments. It made me uncomfortable at times. I could not ignore it. It needed me to breathe life into it. I didn't realize that as I wrote, it was breathing life into me as well (you see, the relationship between author and work is symbiotic).

There were days when I was elated to be carrying the concepts, the words, the sentences living and moving in me. I was grateful and honored that God had entrusted me with its message and was eager to bring it forth. But as it grew, I found myself grappling with it, challenged by the shape it was taking. It didn't look, feel, sound like I thought it should. I questioned, "God, am I hearing You correctly? Is *this* the book?" I wondered if readers would understand. Wondered if it would meet the expectations or needs of its intended audience. Wondered if it would be…enough.

Then I heard one little word: *surrender*. I realized that had to be my posture as both worshiper and writer. I found myself whispering, "Be it unto me according to Your word" and I surrendered, allowing the work to guide me, to inform me, to shape me, to transform me.

We can choose the book we want to write or allow the book that cries to be written to choose us. The very thought that this book has chosen me fills me with a sense of awe. It is God's gift to me and now I offer it back to Him as I offer it to you. Yes, I grappled with it, I battled with it, I argued with it, and it has won out. I am immensely grateful that it has. I present it to you as an encouragement to listen to the voice within you and heed the call. I pray you will be even more inspired to follow that voice as it leads you to a God-designed glorious end. No matter where you find yourself on the writing spectrum, I believe if this book has reached your hands, it is for you.

I pray you sense the heart of the Father on each page, and as you read, you will allow Him to guide you, to inform you, to shape you, to transform you into the writer He has created you to be.

A Writer's Prayer

Heavenly Father, I acknowledge You as Creator of all things.
All good and perfect gifts come from You!
I thank You for the creative gifts You have deposited in me as one created in Your image.
Thank You, Father, for choosing me as a writer to co-create with You.
I submit the gift to You! Use me and use the gift of writing to enable others to see Your glory.
I thank You that You are the One who brings inspiration and ideas through Your Holy Spirit.
Breathe life into each word.
May all that I write be expressions of divine thought.
May each word encourage, enrich and empower all who read them.
May Your love, light, and life be manifested in and through each word, each sentence, each paragraph.

This is my song of worship to You!
In Jesus' Name

My heart bursts its banks, spilling beauty and goodness. I pour it out in a poem to the King, shaping the river into words.
Psalm 45:1 The Message

Introduction:

A Worshiper's Writing Journey

*Thus says the L*ORD*, the God of Israel, 'Write all the words which I have spoken to you in a book.'*
Jeremiah 30:2 NASB

In the living room of our house on Davies Place, right next to the stone fireplace, sat the big green easy chair that my father would settle in each evening after a day of work. On the table nearby, there was always a stack of reading fare: *The Cincinnati Post*, the latest issues of *Ebony* and *Life* magazines, even a collection of Shakespearean sonnets and, of course, the Bible. It was from that chair, sitting on my father's lap, that I began a love affair with words.

My father would read to me with his mesmerizing baritone voice, and whether from the Bible or my favorite collection of fairy tales, he had an exceptional way of placing flesh and bones on the words and calling them to life. I could see the Big Bad Wolf as he huffed and he puffed; I could see each little pig make his great escape by the hairs of his "chinny chin chin." And every time Daddy read 1 Corinthians 13, I would cry.

Listening to my father read spawned in me a love for words and an appreciation for the power they possess. I was fascinated by the idea that someone, having found the precise combination of words, could open my imagination, transport me to worlds beyond my physical borders, make me laugh, or even bring me to tears. I could see the invisible, be touched in the deepest places of my soul, gain new perspectives, expand my mind, enlarge my heart—all through words written on a page! And by age eight, I knew what I wanted to do. I wanted to write.

I've always believed writing is God's gift to me, that He wired me to write. It's always felt organic. It was, and remains, my way of processing my world. It is my most effective way of communicating. It is what gives my ideas voice. It is as natural to me as breathing, and it fills me with such joy.

In college, I majored in Communication Arts with a concentration in journalism. Concern for my financial security prompted my father to have a heart-to-heart talk with me my junior year. "You are a good writer, but you know, it's really difficult to make a living as a writer. Writers can go for years without selling their work. If you teach, you'll have job security and the summers off. You can still write." And so I took the courses necessary for certification in Language Arts and English literature. I had visions of a summer home off the coast of Maine where I'd churn out book after book during vacations. Ahh, the optimism of youth!

When I graduated, I landed a teaching job. The steps that led into the classroom were divinely ordered by God; teaching was a part of His plan for me. As I focused on teaching seventh graders to write, my personal writing became less a priority. I still wrote but with no real thought of publishing. I had journals and notebooks filled with stories, poems, thoughts from conversations with God. I started a newsletter at the church I'd grown up in. But I have to admit I was too afraid to put myself out there by sending manuscripts to agents or publishers or to even submit short pieces to magazines. What if I really had no talent? What if all I received was rejection? What if…?

"What if?" halts so many of us, keeps us from fulfilling our dreams and, even worse, may keep us from fully living out our God-ordained destiny. I don't regret those years of teaching; they were a part of my ordered steps and were gratifying on multiple levels. But as gratifying as they were, there remained a gnawing inside and a knowing that there was more. Writing was a part of the more, but I had allowed fear, doubt and insecurity to keep me from fully embracing one of the ways in which God desired to be glorified and through which I would find greater fulfillment.

Dive Deeper

In 1987, the Lord began speaking to me about worship. Nearly twenty years later, after having led worship and having taught workshops on the subject, I was challenged by my pastor, John W. Stevenson, who has traveled the world teaching on and leading worship. "Deborah," he said, "we need to press in to gain a greater revelation on worship. I believe that there is so much more the Father wants to show us." And as I went deeper, Holy Spirit began to expand my understanding of worship, connecting it with the image of God in us, the glory of God revealed through us, and our gifts, our purposes, our identity, our destiny. This beautiful intertwining helped me see writing within the context of worship.

I began to see worship as a multifaceted diamond of great weight and clarity. The brightest shine is produced as we live our lives in purpose, in love and in obedience to God. The gifts and talents that God has deposited in us are to be used as expressions of worship that allow us to honor God in ways that are authentic, and that allow us to express our love and obedience through every area of life. Teaching is one facet for me; writing is another. And God receives the greatest glory when He is allowed to shine through both.

If I were to walk out purpose and destiny as God intended and honor Him, I had to change my thinking about writing. I'd have to conquer the fears, doubts and insecurities that stopped me. I'd have to silence the voices of Perfectionism and Comparison and begin to speak what God said about me as a writer. I had to rethink my "What ifs" and recognize that, ultimately, I write to honor God.

Step into the F.L.O.W.

You may be one who believes God is speaking to you to write. You may be one who has started writing but found yourself stuck in the mire of doubt and fear. Maybe you have always had a passion for writing but have never fully understood how God desires to use that passion for His glory. *Finding Your F.L.O.W.* is my invitation to you! An invitation to explore writing through the eyes of a worshiper. An invitation to change your thinking about both worship and writing. An invitation to confront the mental barriers, fears and doubts that are preventing you from giving life to the books in you. An invitation to create habits that can move you toward writing success. An invitation to step fully into the *F.L.O.W.*

Each section begins with a personal reflection on writing to inspire you and cause you to think, followed by a discussion of the role of Faith, Love, Obedience, Worship (F.L.O.W.) in the life of Kingdom writers. Each section ends with tips that will help you find your writing flow. The "Write Here, Write Now" sections scattered throughout give opportunity to reflect, to write, and to plan. I believe if you commit to following the tips and completing the exercises, you will prime that creative pump within you so you can begin (or continue) your writing journey.

Prayerfully and worshipfully read each page, believing that as you read Holy Spirit is speaking to the writer in you. As He speaks, change your thinking about the God of infinite possibilities who lives in you and desires for you to co-labor with Him in the creative process. Change your thinking about yourself and see the writer God has called you to be.

Embrace writing as an act of worship, and then…

Write. Write daily. Write soft and easy. Write hard and furiously. Write passionately! Write honestly. Write incessantly! Write in the joy, write through the pain. Write when words flow like honey, write through the dry, barren places. Eventually you will find that oasis, that gushing well. Eventually you will find your *F.L.O.W.*

Write Here, Write Now

> *It's the writing, not the being read, that excites me. Joy is in the doing.*
> Virginia Woolf

What are your earliest memories of writing? How does writing make you feel (happy, alive, anxious, overwhelmed)? Why do you write or want to write? Be as detailed and descriptive as possible.

Do you believe that now, more than any other time in your life, is the time for you to share your story? Why now? What are your writing goals?

Writing as Worship

In Him also we have obtained an inheritance, being predestined according to the purpose of Him who works all things according to the counsel of His will, that we who first trusted in Christ should be to the praise of His glory.

Ephesians 1:11-12

Reflection: A Call to Worship

To me the greatest pleasure of writing is not what it's about, but the inner music the words make.
Truman Capote

It's early morning—just after dawn. As I shuffle to my writing place, I can hear the faint sound of worship music playing. A sliver of sunlight slices through the slit of the still-drawn draperies. Cradling the warm coffee mug in my left hand, I sit, open the sketchbook that I've dubbed as my journal and begin. The sound of my pen gliding across the page is melodious and, though my lips are motionless and not even a hint of a whisper escapes them, I know I have entered a place of prayer, a place of worship. And there is an even deeper knowing that God delights in this moment.

There is no need to write anything profound. No need to inspire or impress. The very act of writing fills me with awe and wonder. As I sit and write, He fills the space. I sense His presence. I smile.

This is a holy place.

There is an exchange. Life flows. I am strengthened and refreshed. Suddenly I realize that this is my authentic act of worship. Words poured out in ink on page are as much my song of adoration and honor as notes I play on a keyboard or melodies that cascade from my lips!

I can't help but wonder if those things that I find myself giving undue attention to during the course of my days and weeks pull me away from moments like this, pull me from my Center, draw me from Him. I can't help but wonder if, just perhaps, the voices that tell me that I don't have time, or this is nothing more than a hobby, that there are more pressing matters to attend to or that I am, at best, a mediocre writer are no more than subtle, yet intentional, ploys of the enemy to steal time away from God. I wonder if by not making writing a greater priority in my life how many hallowed moments like this I have missed. Maybe these are the times that touch His heart most deeply. Maybe this is one of my greatest declarations of love.

I wonder how often we are drawn away from the very thing that God is longing for because we fail to reverence it as holy to the Lord, fail to see it as an act of worship. I wonder why we don't allow ourselves greater opportunity to honor God with all He has given us as expressions of authentic worship.

The act of writing is an act of worship. Writing for a writer is as much worship as singing is to a singer, dancing is to a dancer, painting is to a painter, mothering is to a mother, teaching is to a teacher, even as building a business and creating wealth are to an entrepreneur. It's our holy incense billowing to God's nostrils, giving Him pleasure!

Creativity lives in all of us because we are created in the image and likeness of *the* Creator. Not only that, we were created as worshipers, and the two—worship and creativity—are inextricably linked. Creativity is woven into the very fiber of the worshiper's being. To stifle or suppress it, to deny or diminish it, to minimize or marginalize it is to deny a part of who we are as image bearers and worshipers. When we are unable or unwilling to use the gifts that have been seared into our creative DNA, we sense something lacking in our lives. God has uniquely gifted and graced us to fulfill purpose in our own unique way—some through the creation of music, others the creation of art, others through the building of wealth, and others through the written word. It is when we fully engage, develop, nurture and exercise those gifts and talents that we feel most connected to the Creator, we feel a greater sense of oneness with Him. We feel a greater sense of wholeness. We feel alive!

American author Joseph Chilton Pearce wrote, "We must accept that this creative pulse within us is God's creative pulse itself." Could it be that when we fail to employ our creative side—no matter how it manifests in and through us—our hearts miss a beat? And could it be that each time that happens, we lose a bit of that which pumps life and purpose into us and we are slightly out of rhythm with the very heartbeat of God?

Something almost supernatural happens when I find my writing flow—the place where my spirit is so completely one with His. It's then that I know I have found what Wright Morris calls the soul's "Great Good Place." I am energized! Words ooze from my core. I am in my grace zone and I am free! It is like coming home to a place that not only fills me with love, light, and life, but also allows me to become an expression His love, light, and life in the earth. I want to stay in that place, to live in that place, to live *from* that place. I can no longer be content to wander its perimeters. I believe there are many—like you—with that same desire. It is my prayer that together we will step into that flow as we embrace writing as worship.

Write Here, Write Now

> *Writers have an island, a center of refuge, within themselves. It is the mind's anchorage, the soul's Great Good Place.*
> Wright Morris

What is your "Great Good Place" or your grace zone? Write about a time when you were in that place. What were you doing? Where were you? How did it feel? Be as detailed as possible, as if you are reliving the moment. What can you do to have more "Great Good Place" moments?

What are your authentic expressions of worship?

DEBORAH A. GASTON

The Worship-Writing Connection

To create is to be human.
To create is to fulfill our divine intention.
To create is to reflect the image of God.
To create is an act of worship.
Erwin Raphael McManus *The Artisan Soul*

"Writing as worship?" my friend murmured. It was as if the words were rolling around in her head, trying to find a place to lodge and put down roots, but there was no compartment or category, no box into which the idea neatly fit. "I've never heard that before," she continued. "Can you explain what you mean?"

It's a common response. It may have even been your response when you first read the words, and, it is understandable. The word "worship" has different connotations depending on our worship paradigm, our context, our teaching, our personal and corporate worship experience. Even now as you are reading, you have placed worship in a certain framework, and depending on that framework, you will readily grasp the ideas in this book, or you may be challenged by them. If your worship context is rooted in specific types of expression, then to place writing, in all its various forms, in that same context may be difficult.

We must change our thinking and begin to see worship in a broader context than many have been taught. I believe for the Christian who has a desire to write understanding worship is essential. When we open our hearts and expand our understanding of what it means to be a worshiper and what true worship can look like, we are able to see worship in ways that relate to our identity and our purpose. A simple shift in perspective may impact how we live out purpose and destiny as our worship expression expands. That simple shift in thinking may cause us to approach all of life, and subsequently writing, differently as we see it all as worship.

Write Here, Write Now

> *It is the pleasing of God that is at the heart of worship.*
> R.C. Sproul

Before we begin to reshape our view of worship, take a moment to define worship in your own words. What does it look like? What does it feel like? Does it have a sound? When do you know you've engaged in true worship? What, if anything, does it accomplish? What does it mean to give God glory? What has shaped your definition of worship?

Describe a specific worship encounter that changed you. Write in detail about the place, the people, what you heard, saw, felt. How did it impact you?

Worship Re-imagined

It's who you are and the way you live that count before God. Your worship must engage your spirit in the pursuit of truth. That's the kind of people the Father is out looking for: those who are simply and honestly themselves before him in their worship. God is sheer being itself—Spirit. Those who worship him must do it out of their very being, their spirits, their true selves, in adoration.

John 4:23,24 The Message

"We were not created to worship God." This is opening sentence of John W. Stevenson's book, *Worshiper by Design: A Unique Look at Why We Were Created*. (And yes, I could see you bristling as you read those words). Stevenson goes on to explain that God did not create us to *do* worship but to *be* worshipers, and from our *being* flows that which we *do*. Stevenson writes:

> Adam was not created to worship God, but as a worshiper. All that he was called to do—from having dominion to tending the garden to naming the animals—was to flow from that state of being. And so it is with us; for you see, man was created to be, not to do! **We were not designed to do worship, but we were designed to be worshipers**[1] (emphasis added).

Adam was a worshiper and from him flowed expressions or acts of worship. In what ways did Adam worship? We have no indication from scripture that he sang or danced, neither are we privy to the conversations he may have had with his Creator as they walked in the Garden in the cool of the day. As wonderful as I imagine those times were, I do not believe they were Adam's ultimate expression of worship. His expression of worship was evidenced in a life of love and obedience to God by *being* who God had created him to be and by *doing* all God had commissioned him to do. The hymn of praise that swelled from Adam's life was composed through tending the Garden, through naming the animals, through lovingly and obediently living out Genesis 1:28 as he remained connected to the Father.

And *you* were created as a worshiper. Stevenson defines a worshiper as "one who is intimately acquainted with and has a daily relationship with God exhibited through obedience."[2] You were created to be in relationship with the Father, and that relationship is one of intimacy, constancy, and obedience. From that intimacy, constancy and obedience flow expressions of worship that are aligned with who you are (identity) and why you were created (purpose). I believe that these are the expressions that allow God to get the maximum glory from our lives.

What is true worship? And how does it find expression in our lives beyond song, dance and words of love and adoration to God? There are many definitions, but for the sake of common ground and understanding, let's develop a definition that will enable us to see all of life as worship in general, and writing as worship, in particular.

Worship can best be defined as that which flows from the life of one who has an intimate relationship with God, who has learned to hear His voice and obey. Every act of love and obedience in response to our God and to His Word is an act of worship. Every faith response to God is an act of worship. I may tell God how much I love Him in a song, in a dance, in a prayer. But the ultimate expression of love is not in what I say or sing, but in a life lived in fulfillment of that which He has spoken. When I obey, I worship!

Worship is our loving, obedient response to a revelation from God, and our worship response may be expressed in a myriad of ways that acknowledge and honor Him. Our greatest act of worship is *being* all He intended us be, expressing His life through the gifts—spiritual and natural—He has deposited in us as we walk out purpose and destiny.

Remember Who You Are

We have become his poetry, a re-created people that will fulfill the destiny he has given each of us, for we are joined to Jesus, the Anointed One. Even before we were born, God planned in advance our destiny and the good works we would do to fulfill it!

Ephesians 2:10 TPT

A few years ago I was asked to speak on worship at a women's retreat. As I prepared, the Lord spoke these words, "Remind them who they are! Remind them that they are worshipers." There were women from all over the country in attendance—wives, mothers, daughters, pastors, students, entrepreneurs. God wanted them to know that before they were any of those things, they were worshipers and all else had to flow from that truth. I found myself writing these words in my notes: *I am not a worshiper because I worship; I worship because I am a worshiper.*

We live in a culture that seeks to define us by what we do. But our identity is not determined by what we do; our identity in Christ *determines* what we do. I am a teacher. I am not a teacher because I teach; I teach because I am a teacher. My education and training, and 30 years in a classroom didn't make me a teacher. It is who God created me to be, and even if I hadn't worked in public schools, teaching would still be something I do because at the core of my *being*, I am a teacher.

I am not a writer because I write; I write because I am a writer. If I never published another book or created another blog post, I would still write in some form because at the core of my *being*, I am a writer. And since I was created as a worshiper who is also a teacher and a writer, my greatest expressions of worship are seen when I do that which flows from who I am—teach and write.

Who are you? What expressions of worship flow from who you are at your core? Life in Christ is a journey of discovering who God created you to be and how He has purposed for you to reflect His image by simply *being* who He says you are. What flows from you then becomes your authentic worship to Him.

He created you to be, among other things, a writer! Now worship Him! Write!

Write Here, Write Now

The act of writing is an act of worship. Writing for a writer is as much worship as singing is to a singer, dancing is to a dancer, painting is to a painter, mothering is to a mother, teaching is to a teacher, even as building a business and creating wealth are to an entrepreneur. It's our holy incense billowing to His nostrils, giving Him pleasure!

Respond to the statement above. In light of what you now know, what changes might you make so that your life is even more reflective of the true worshiper you are?

How will you fit writing into this new paradigm? What are some of the other facets of your worship diamond?

DEBORAH A. GASTON

Create a Writing Worship Practice through Journaling

Journal writing is a voyage to the interior.
Christina Baldwin

Worshipers become intimately acquainted with God because of the daily relationship they have with Him. True intimacy is not born out of casualness, nor is it born out of convenience. Intentional time in worship, prayer, time in the Word, time waiting in His presence and listening for His voice are essential in growing to know the Lord in deeper, richer, more intimate ways.

Writers become writers because they spend time writing. Good writing is not born out of casualness, out of convenience, nor through osmosis. Writers become good writers (and good writers become better) because they are intentional about writing! They develop a discipline around writing, which means even if they are not working on a specific project, they still write. If we are to produce what God is speaking to us, if we are to be obedient to the call, we cannot be casual in our approach. We find our flow by creating and maintaining a writing practice.

Many successful authors speak of the importance of creating a daily writing practice. As we explore writing as worship, I want to suggest that you create and maintain a *writing worship* practice by incorporating writing in your devotional time. This is an intentional time to journal, to free write, to reflect, to breathe onto paper, and empty your heart and mind of whatever thoughts are nestling there (or wrestling there). This is a time of asking God questions, listening for His response and writing what you hear. This is time with God, sacred, worshipful, transforming.

I've been journaling for more years than I can count. It is through journaling that I hear God speak most clearly. My relationship with Him has been strengthened as a result. My journal is the place I can be my truest self, the place I reveal my soul. Not only has journaling strengthened my relationship with God, I found it has helped me to grow as a writer. In fact, my first book, *God Speaks: Words for the Journey from the Father's Heart,* is really nothing more than journal entries.

I am not alone in my belief that journaling is one of the best ways to grow as a writer. Both writers and psychologists believe there are many benefits to journaling from releasing stress to sparking creativity to improving memory. One very significant benefit is that journaling helps us know ourselves better. For the worshiper who writes, a journal can become a book of prayers, a book of psalms, a book of revelation.

For the writer, a journal is not only a place to keep ideas but can help generate them. Free writing, a form of stream of consciousness[3] writing, serves several wonderful purposes for the writer. In addition to generating ideas, free writing can hurl you over writer's block, and free your mind of the thoughts and emotions that serve as distractors and cause you to lose focus. This kind of writing can be healing and liberating as well. It is a place where you are free to make mistakes, to explore, to be inspired because there are no rules, and nothing is off limits.

All you need to begin is a notebook and pen. Neither need be expensive or fancy—it's all a matter of personal preference. Place both journal and pen where you can readily access them. You never know when an idea will beg to be given expression or when God will speak to you.

I suggest that you use pen and paper rather than a computer or tablet. Research has shown that the physical act of writing brings information to the forefront of the brain and triggers it to pay attention. Maud Purcell writes in her article "The Health Benefits of Journaling":

> The act of writing accesses your left brain, which is analytical and rational. While your left brain is occupied, your right brain is free to create, intuit and feel. In sum, writing removes mental blocks and allows you to use all of your brainpower to better understand yourself, others and the world around you."[4]

Studies have also shown that those who write their text rather than type, write more words and express more ideas.

Here are a few more journaling guidelines that will help you:
- Pray! For the believer, writing is a collaborative effort with Holy Spirit.
- Date everything. You'll be able to go back and see growth and transformation.
- Set a time limit. If you're new to journaling and free writing, you may want to begin with 5 minutes and gradually increase the time. Aim for a minimum of 15-20 minutes a day.
- You may decide to write on a specific topic or use a prompt like the ones throughout this book to get you started. You may just want to begin writing and see what emerges. Even if you have to repeat the same thing over and over until the creative pump is primed and words and ideas begin to flow freely, that's OK. The words and ideas will come if you just keep writing.
- Write your first thoughts! Frances Bacon said, "Write down the thoughts of the moment. Those that come unsought, for they are commonly the most valuable." Not only are they the most valuable, they are the most honest. Do not censor yourself. This is the place where you can be honest, vulnerable and raw.
- Don't stop writing! The goal is to become fluid. Keep writing until the time is up.
- Don't edit! This is not about "correctness." It's about getting ideas, feelings and observations on paper. So don't concern yourself with spelling, grammar, punctuation, syntax. JUST WRITE!

Go back at some point and read what you've written. Circle words, phrases and ideas that are crying to be more fully developed, and then set aside time to flesh out those ideas. You'll be amazingly surprised at what you discover about God, about yourself, about the world around you and the world within you.

And who knows? There may be a book amid the ramblings.

Write Here, Write Now

> *Fill your paper with the breathings of your heart.*
> William Wordsworth

Now is the time to begin. Get your journal or notebook. Place today's date at the top of the page. Set the timer on your phone for 5 minutes and just write until the timer goes off. If you're in the middle of a thought when the timer buzzes, complete the thought.

Now read what you've written. Are there ideas that can be further developed? Highlight or circle them.

Take time to pray about the ideas you highlighted. What is Holy Spirit speaking to you? Set aside time to further develop those ideas.

Faith

By faith, we see the world called into existence by God's word, what we see created by what we don't see.

Hebrews 11:3 The Message

Reflection: On Being a Kingdom Writer

I am a Christian. Not in a religious kind of way. Not in "follow-a list-of-do's-and-don'ts" kind of way. Beyond where I go and what I do on Sunday mornings (or where I don't go and what I don't do on Saturday nights). Beyond all the stuff—positive and negative—that many associate with Christians and Christianity. I am Christian because I identify with Jesus Christ, with His life, death, burial, resurrection. I believe He is who He says He is. I believe He accomplished all He said He did. I believe He did it because He loves me. I believe He did it *for* me. I believe He did it *as* me.

I am a Christian because I am learning daily to let go of the person that I believed myself to be and fully embrace my true identity in Christ. I am allowing His Spirit to transform me. In Him I live, move, have my very existence. I have invited Him to express His life in and through me. Christian is as much a part of me as inhale/exhale.

I am a Writer. Not in the "New-York-Times-Bestseller-List" kind of way (at least not yet). Not in the full-time job, "if-I-don't-write, I-don't-eat" kind of way. Beyond a list of accomplishments that might legitimize me as Writer in the eyes of others. Definitely beyond an income indicative of large book sales or thousands of blog followers. It is part of my identity. It was woven into my DNA by my Creator. I didn't wake up one day and think, "I'll be a writer." The writer was awakened in me by the One Who planted the desire in my heart. Writing is a source of fulfillment, joy, satisfaction. Writing lives, moves, has its being in me. It is my heart cry, my soul-speak, my prayer language. It is almost as vital to me as inhale/exhale.

I am a writer who is a Christian! I am a Christian writer. I cannot extricate one from the other.

I am not a Christian writer because I write of "Christian" things. I am not a Christian writer because every blog post, article, story or book directly points my reader to the cross of Christ (though I pray my work reveals the loving heart of God). If I write a love poem or a story that doesn't mention Father, Son or Holy Spirit, if I script a play in the Lorraine Hansberry tradition, create a fantasy world like Narnia, if I don't quote one passage of scripture, I am still a Christian writer.

I am a Christian writer because of what I believe to be true about God. Those beliefs are the bedrock of all I am and all I do; they are the force that determines how I choose to live and choose to write. What I believe to be true about Him serves as the foundation from which I write what I write within a large spectrum of subjects.

I am a Christian writer because my relationship with Christ enables me to see life through different lenses and from a higher perspective. It doesn't matter what genre or subject. All of life is open for exploration because I believe the truth in the psalmist's words: "The earth is the Lord's and all its fullness, the world and those who dwell therein. For He has founded it upon the seas and established it upon the water" (Psalm 24:1,2). It all belongs to Him and it is all a writer's fare.

My relationship with the One who created it all and my faith rooted in His truth form the compass that guides me. Kingdom principles, Biblical truths are the underpinning of all I do. My relationship with Christ empowers me to write from a mindset shaped by faith in all that God says is true. I write from a Kingdom perspective. I bring that Kingdom perspective into every area of life, recognizing that perhaps the call to write is a commission from God to bring His glory to that which has been stamped as unholy, to shine His light upon that which has been perverted and to allow others to see from a new perspective.

I believe that the line between sacred and secular is nebulous at best. It is a line that Satan uses to claim territory that, by all rights, belongs to God. If Satan has perverted literature, film, the arts, we don't simply surrender them to him. We take them back! We make them holy and sacred once again as we allow Holy Spirit within us to breath into us words that are real, words that are honest, words that are engaging and entertaining, but that do not bring ungodly images to the mind of the reader or stir up ungodly desires. We allow Holy Spirit to breathe life into each word, transforming our work into that which honors the Father.

Holy Spirit is the Compass. He is the Censor. I am the scribe.

Perhaps "Christian" writer is a misnomer. Above all, I am a citizen of the Kingdom of God. I am a Kingdom Writer, commissioned to enable others to see life through a new lens—the lens of Love.

Write Here, Write Now

Now I want you to write what you have seen, what is, and what will be after the things that I reveal to you.
Revelation 1:19 TPT

Sit still and listen. Then journal your response to the following questions.

What does it mean for you be called as a Kingdom writer? What is your responsibility to God, to your readers, and to yourself? What is God revealing to you that you want to write about?

Take some to time free write about the story or insight you want to share with others.

An Act of Faith, An Act of Worship

> *"Because you're not yet taking God seriously," said Jesus. "The simple truth is that if you had a mere kernel of faith, a poppy seed, say, you would tell this mountain, 'Move!' and it would move. There is nothing you wouldn't be able to tackle."*
>
> Matthew 17:20 MSG

Seven women had gathered. Seven women of faith who love of God. Seven women seeking to connect, to encourage and to be encouraged, to nudge and to be nudged. Seven worshipers invited by God to change the world through the written word. Seven women who had accepted the invitation. At the end of the table that was covered with laptops and tablets, with cups of coffee or tea, sat the newest member to our group.

"I'm not really a writer," she began, almost embarrassed by the confession. I smiled and when she finished, said, "Maybe you simply need to change what you say." She looked at me quizzically. I continued, "Well, we know there is power in our words."

Then I said to my "not-really-a-writer" friend, "Maybe the truth is that up until now you didn't know there was a writer in you. So now you just need to declare what God is calling you in this season of your life. Begin by saying, 'I am a writer!'"

She looked at me, smiled, nodded, and the other women who had gathered gave a collective nod, followed by verbal affirmation.

"*I am a writer!*" Do you find those words difficult to say? It may challenge you because you, like many writers, are plagued with doubt and fear and all the questions that doubt and fear breed: *Do I really have any talent? Do I really have something worth saying? Will anyone even care what I have to say? Can I live up to other's expectations? Can I live up to my own expectations? What if I allow myself to be vulnerable on paper and people judge or reject me? What if people discover I'm a fraud?* These thoughts will cause you to question if you can do what your heart is telling you.

You can do it. It doesn't matter if you have not published anything yet. It doesn't matter if, until now, you've spent more time thinking about writing than you have actually spent writing. It doesn't matter if you have boxes of notes and unfinished manuscripts that you just can't seem to complete. It doesn't matter if every time you sit to write, you have flashbacks of the English teacher who bled red ink all over the essay you poured your heart into and slapped the word "REWRITE" in bold letters across the top, convincing you that you have no skill or talent. It doesn't even matter if you failed English.

All that matters is this moment and the decision you are making now—the decision to write! You must own who you are called to be by faith and come into agreement with what God is saying about you as a writer. And if you are reading this book, then God is calling forth the writer in you in this season of your life. He has created you as a worshiper who writes. Finding your writing flow begins by believing in your heart and aligning your thoughts with what God is saying to you concerning writing. As you think in your heart, you are (Proverbs 23:7).

As an act of faith, make this declaration: *I am a writer!*

Faith: A Prerequisite for Writing

Writing is an act of faith, not a trick of grammar.
E.B. White

Faith is essential in the life of the writer, just as it is in the life of the believer. You must have faith that God has called and equipped you as a writer. You must have faith that the burning desire to share your story, to share some insight, to teach or to entertain has been planted in you by the One who gives you the desires of your heart (Psalm 37:4). You must have faith in the creative ability you possess as one created in His image. You must believe that Holy Spirit will speak to you, inspiring and directing you as you commit to co-create with Him. You must believe that as you diligently seek Him, He will reward you with the words, the sentences, the paragraphs, the books that enable you to fulfill the dream He has placed in your heart. You must have faith that what you write—regardless of genre—will impact others. You must have faith that someone is waiting to read the words that only you can pen.

Faith is a prerequisite. It takes faith to pick up the pen and write!

Webster's New World Dictionary defines faith as "confidence or trust in a person or a thing." Our confidence is in the Lord, not in our gifts, our abilities, our education. We are to live all our life by a faith rooted in Jesus Christ, the Originator of our faith; all faith begins and is completed in Him (Hebrews 12:2). When we learn to live from His faith and trust in His faithfulness to fulfill His word, then we find that we really can do more than we've ever imagined.

God has chosen you—even though you may still be grappling with the notion that there is a writer inside you. You have something to say that only you can say. You have been called as a Kingdom writer for such as time as this.

God has called you because He believes in you. He knows what He has deposited in you. He is calling it to life and all He asks of you is to trust what He knows about you—trust and then cooperate. He never asks anything of you without providing for you. That means not only has He already provided the ideas, the concepts, the stories, He has also provided the faith and the grace you need to write. The Apostle Paul wrote, "...the life which I now live in the flesh I live **by the faith of the Son of God,** who loved me and gave Himself for me" (Galatians 2:20 emphasis added). We live (and write) by His faith, knowing that what He has spoken, He will perform, and knowing that He has chosen to collaborate with you!

Life in Christ is a life of dependence on Him for everything. He desires to do all of life with and through us. He wants us to simply choose to *not* do life without Him, but allow His faith within us to be the source from which we live—and from which we write.

You must remember this: faith is not demonstrated by what we *say* we believe; it is demonstrated by our actions. That is what we read in James—faith without corresponding action is useless. I like the Mirror Bible translation of James 2:18:

> Faith is not in competition with works; the one cannot operate without the other. ***Faith remains invisible without action; indeed, the only way to communicate faith is in doing the things prompted and inspired by faith***[5] (emphasis added).

Remember, all acts of worship are acts of faith as we respond worshipfully, lovingly and obediently to a revelation from God. And for the writer that worshipful, loving, obedient response is the act of writing.

The Fear Factor

You can, you should, and if you're brave enough to start, you will.
Stephen King

Novice writers may often think that they are the only ones who struggle with fear. Fear is no respecter of person and even the most accomplished writers contend with it. You and I may face it every time we sit to write. Steven Pressfield writes in *The War of Art*: "Are you paralyzed with fear? That's a good sign. Fear is good. Like self-doubt, fear is an indicator. Fear tells us what we have to do. Remember one rule of thumb: the more scared we are of a work or calling, the more sure we can be that we have to do it." [6]

Fear and doubt may be a part of every writer's journey, but every writer has a choice in how he or she responds to them. We must choose not to run from them. We must be willing to face them, to stare them down, to command them to go! And if they persist, we must be courageous enough to write through them, write over them, write around them, write because of them, write despite them. We must remind ourselves of Paul's words in 2 Timothy 1:7 and make those words our own daily confession: "For God has not given us a spirit of fear, but of power and of love and of a sound mind." As believers, we know we have an enemy who, in the subtlest of ways, tries to undermine our faith and trust in order to move us away from our Center. He does this by attempting to convince us that the truth we have come to believe is not truth at all. He brings distractions into our lives to reroute our focus so we lose sight of God and our God-ordained purposes and destiny.

This is true of every believer; this is true of every writer.

I am convinced that, as writers, our biggest challenge is overcoming the thoughts that so often taunt us. These thoughts are the breeding ground for fear and every other enemy associated with it, especially doubt. Doubt may be a writer's most insidious enemy. It causes us to question, and it can paralyze us if we don't confront it. When we listen to the voice of doubt, we procrastinate at best or don't try at all.

Doubt often manifests in what author Sue Monk Kidd refers to as the "internal backlash of fear" or in the voices of our "inner critics." We all have them, and each time we sit to produce, they speak softly to us to negate the truth of who we are in Christ, who we are as worshipers and who we are as writers. If we listen to them, we will make choices that move us farther and farther away from our goals and dreams. They may even convince us that our destiny lies in something else altogether. We will never produce anything worthwhile. We will not produce fruit that remains long after we have transitioned from this life. We will never impact generations as we are intended. We must identify those critics, stare them down and render them speechless. If they refuse to be silenced, we must choose to ignore them and write anyway.

Paul tells us that we are transformed by the renewing of our minds. He writes:
> Stop imitating the ideals and opinions of the culture around you, but be inwardly transformed by the Holy Spirit through a total reformation of how you think. This will empower you to discern God's will as you live a beautiful life, satisfying and perfect in his eyes.[7] (Romans 12: 2,3 TPT)

The word "transformed" is the Greek word *metamorphoo*, meaning a total change. It's a change that begins in our thinking and is evidenced in our behavior. Pushing past fear and doubt to create what is in us requires that we think of ourselves the way God thinks of us. His thoughts become our thoughts as we acknowledge that we have the mind of Christ (1 Corinthians 2:16) and nothing is impossible because we believe (Matthew 17:20; Luke 1:37).

He calls you Writer! He desires to co-create with you! Trust in His faithfulness to fulfill His word in your life as a writer!

Write Here, Write Now

If you want to write, you can. Fear stops most people from writing, not lack of talent, whatever that is. Who am I? What right have I to speak? Who will listen to me if I do? You're a human being, with a unique story to tell, and you have every right. If you speak with passion, many of us will listen. We need stories to live, all of us. We live by story. Yours enlarges the circle.
Richard Rhodes

Take 60 seconds and list those things that have made you doubt yourself as a writer. What does that inner critic whisper to you that causes your faith as a writer to wane?

Then write a letter to the writer in you, encouraging your writer self and countering the fears, doubts and lies with declarations of faith and truth.

Whenever the inner critics rear their heads, read your letter aloud and then…WRITE!

Faith and Vulnerability

> *If writing is honest it cannot be separated from the man who wrote it.*
> Tennessee Williams

For the writer (and perhaps for all artists), fear has two faces and we must conquer both in order to produce. Fear can become an impetus that pushes us to create our best work. We learn to use fear to our advantage; we learn to produce in its presence. And as we do, the voices begin to abate until they no longer have any influence. We become fearless and a writing force that cannot be ignored.

There is a kind of fearlessness that writers must possess that enables us to push past places of comfort, places of safety and, in some cases, places of hiding. I'm not talking about just those fears we easily identify: the fear of failure, the fear of rejection, the fear of not being good enough, or even fear of success. I'm referring to the fear of emptying ourselves on the page. We cannot be safe and be truly impactful. We cannot hide ourselves from ourselves or from our audience and touch souls deeply. Allowing ourselves to be vulnerable is the place of authentic worship, and it is the place of authentic writing. We are open, we are honest, and we allow our honesty to lead us to truth. Our readers willingly follow because we have invited them into our hearts, into the depths of our souls. We have dared to say, "This is who I am—the good, the not-so-good, the beautiful and the ugly. This is the weak and the strong of me. This is the imperfect self who is learning to let God perfect me." We show them our humanness. Through our writing, we say to all who read, "We are not so different!" As we do, they learn to trust us.

Every time I sit to write, I come face to face with myself. It doesn't matter what I'm writing—whether journaling, blogging, or working on a chapter of the next book. The paper or computer screen becomes a mirror and I have to make decisions. How much of myself am I willing to reflect in the words I pen? How much of myself am I willing to expose? How much of myself am I willing to discover by allowing myself to be exposed and open? Will my readers judge me or embrace me as a result of seeing glimpses of who I really am? How much am I willing to risk, how courageous am I willing to be in order to emerge at the end of the writing encounter more than I am at the moment I begin? These are choices you must make as well.

I know it's not always easy to allow ourselves to be spiritually, mentally and emotionally accessible—even on paper. There are just some things that we don't want to face about ourselves, some things we don't want others to know, the truth behind the wonderfully, carefully constructed image we like to project to the world. If we choose to go deep and write from the very depths of who we are—not who we want people to think we are—several things happen. We find a place of truth. We find a place of healing. We find a place of wholeness. We find a place of freedom. We find grace. And as we discover and reveal the many faces of grace, our readers find those wonderful places as well.

Faith and Freedom

The quill has pricked my soul and each word bleeds into the parchment of my life. My freedom is in my words; therefore, I write.
R. MonaLeza

Finding our writing flow can lead us to places of freedom like none we have experienced if we allow ourselves to be open and willing to embrace truth. Jesus said we'd know truth and the truth we know would make us free (John 8:32). Allowing ourselves to face our fears, to confront the thoughts and feelings of doubt that halt us, giving ourselves permission to be imperfect human beings, revealing our many-faceted selves, and extricating ourselves from all expectations (our own as well as those of others) frees us. Frees us to be led by no other voice than that of the Creative One living inside us. Frees us to explore all of life. Frees us to make mistakes in order to find new avenues of expression. Frees us to discover our authentic selves, the fearfully and wonderfully made individuals and writers God uniquely fashioned us to be. It even frees us to break some rules and to write in ways that may lead others to freedom.

John recorded these words of Christ: "Therefore, if the Son makes you free, you shall be free indeed" (John 8:36). Because Christ has freed us from sin and its effects, we are free to be ourselves, free to see the unlimited possibilities that exist all around us but, more importantly, within us because the God with Whom all things are possible dwells in us, inspiring us.

Worshiper, you are free! Writer, you are free! Declare this as your personal Independence Day! Say good-bye to every fear that has held you hostage, lied to you about who you are, and prevented the words from flowing.

Today you have stepped in a new flow—one of faith, fearlessness and freedom!

Write Here, Write Now

Write what disturbs you, what you fear, what you have been unable to speak. Be willing to be split open.
Natalie Goldberg

What are the truths you've hidden because you feared that others might reject you if they knew? What truths have you been unwilling to face because of fear? What is the one story you'd tell if you knew that by telling it, not only would you be healed and set free, but someone else would as well?

Begin writing that story. Be willing to be split open.

In Search of Inspiration

Writing is about learning to pay attention and to communicate what's going on.
Anne LaMott *Bird by Bird*

There are days that I just don't feel inspired to write. I know I need to crank out a monthly post for my blog or complete a chapter of a work-in-progress, and nothing is flowing. I sit at the computer waiting for inspiration to strike like a bolt of lightning. It never does! I wait, hoping the heavens will open and words will fall like rain. They never do. Sometimes I force myself to write, even if what I write is less than stellar, hoping to find treasure in the trash. More often, I pick up my phone, scroll through my Facebook feed or play a round (or ten) of Candy Crush.

The truth is there will be days when the inspiration to write seems all but gone and we can't manage to push through to get one sentence on a page. Now and then it's perfectly OK to do something…anything but write. Other days you write through the drought. And then there are days you go in search of inspiration.

Inspiration can come from a myriad of places: a word, a phrase, a smile, the sound of laughter, a sermon, a scripture, a bird chirping. Maybe watching your children play or an aroma that reminds you of your childhood. Maybe you hear God speak gently to your spirit as you walk or work out. Inspiration is all around us! It's in us—if we open our hearts, our eyes, our ears and simply pay attention.

One of my favorite reference books is Noah Webster's *The American Dictionary of the English Language* published in 1828. Read Webster's definition of inspiration:
- *the act of breathing into anything*
- *the infusion of ideas into the mind by the Holy Spirit; the conveying into the mind of men ideas…by supernatural influence or the*

communication of the divine will to the understanding by suggestions or impressions on the mind.

Who inspires you? Who is breathing into you? Who is infusing your mind with ideas? Where to do you find the ideas and the impetus to write?

Author Jack London said, "You can't wait for inspiration. You have to go after it with a club." I have learned to go after it! Sometimes it's as simple as a change of routine. Other days taking a walk or changing my environment help. Doing something new is a great source of inspiration—always prayerfully asking Holy Spirit to infuse our hearts and minds and to highlight the things we often pay little attention to that can be sources of inspiration, lessons and insight!

Other sources of inspiration may be found in:
    Reading a book or blog post
    News headlines and stories
    Reading through old journals
    A line in your favorite song
    A scene from a movie or TV show
    A quote
    A sermon
    Listening to music
    Past experiences
    Being still and listening to Holy Spirit speak
    Photos or works of art
    Free writing

I challenge you to go after inspiration (with or without the club) regularly and see what you find. Do something you've never done before or something you've not done for a long time. Go to a museum or a concert in the park. Go to the mall and people watch. Be creative! Be still and allow the One Who breathes into you to communicate with you through new means. Pay attention! Be present to His Presence in a greater way! Pray for greater sensitivity to all that is around you and within you. Then write! You'll be pleasingly surprised.

Write Here, Write Now

> *You can't wait for inspiration. You have to go after it with a club.*
> Jack London

In what ways do you go after inspiration? Make a list of places you've never been or things you've always wanted to do or haven't done in a long time. Then set a date with yourself to try something new and write about it.

Listen to one of your favorite songs. Choose a line from the song and write a story based on the lyrics.

Love

For I know the plans I have for you, says the Lord, plans for your welfare and not for evil, to give you a hope and a future.

Jeremiah 29:11

Reflection: Why I Write

Then He who sat on the throne said, "Behold, I make all things new." And He said to me, "Write, for these words are true and faithful."
Revelation 21:5

Author Flannery O'Connor said, "I write because I don't know what I think until I read what I said." That sentence capsulizes, in part, why I write. As a young girl, I was a bit awkward, quiet, introverted, and writing became my way of making sense of the world without and the world within, and bringing harmony to both worlds. It was my way of taking the insanity of the world and bringing order and meaning to it, or escaping it temporarily. Writing was my way of searching the hills and valleys, scaling the mountains, exploring the caverns, excavating the mines of my soul to discover who I am. To find my place in the scheme of something larger and grander than myself—something that, at times, seemed senseless to me, but was nonetheless magnificent and filled with wonder.

As a child, writing was my way of capturing the joy of birthday parties or Christmases, baking cookies with Mommy, going on excursions with Daddy or the sorrow over the death of a pet, of being among the last to be chosen for a team, of wearing glasses at age eight, of being slightly overweight. Writing was my way of sealing the events of my life within my memory.

As a teen, I wrote to sort out emotions and to empty myself of all the things I felt I just couldn't share with anyone else without being grossly misunderstood. It was a way of spewing out pent-up frustrations, disappointments, anger. A way to capture the moment the cute boy in class looked at me or slipped me a note or an upper classman called me by name. To replay the first the dance, the first kiss, the first love as well as work through the pain of the first twinge of jealousy, the first argument, the first heartbreak. To spill out teen angst in a judgment-free zone. I wrote to give a record, to say I was here in this time and space and this is how I interpreted my world.

Nicole Krauss probably said it best. She wrote: "Why does one begin to write? Because she feels misunderstood, I guess. Because it never comes out clearly enough when she tries to speak. Because she wants to rephrase the world, to take it in and give it back differently, so everything is used, and nothing is lost…"

I write because I love the melodious sound of pen gliding across paper. I love the feeling that fills me as I shape letters into words, words into sentences, forming thoughts that then take on a life of their own—a life and a legacy that I pray will long outlive me. I write because words float in my head and heart, wafting on the breeze of my imagination. I see them, bold and beautiful, soft and sweet, colorful. They float and fly and bounce off each other, looking to connect to express meaning greater than they possess solitarily. They call to me, asking me to give them life, purpose, destiny.

I write, as Flannery O'Connor once said when asked why she writes, because I want to. But beyond that, because I must. It has never been about publishing volumes of work or making a name for myself among the literary greats, or with the hope that one day I would be required reading, and high school juniors would dissect my work and extol my insight into the human condition. It's never been about making a lot of money.

I wrote then and I write now because it is the way God has given me as not only my way to process my world, but as His way of communicating His heart of love with me and then through me. I write to hear God speak. Writing is our way—the Father's and mine—of communicating with one another in the most intimate of ways. It is our love exchange, our love song, our Father-daughter dance and no one else can enter that space of grand intimacy.

I write because it is my sacred and authentic language of love.

Write Here, Write Now

> **Some write because God has spoken; I write to hear Him speak.**
> Unknown

Why do you write? What do you gain from writing? In what ways does it help you, feed you, fulfill you? How does God wish to communicate to you through your writing?

Expressions of Love

> *Those who are loved by God, let his love continually pour from you to one another, because God is love. Everyone who loves is fathered by God and experiences intimate knowledge of him.*
> 1 John 4:7 TPT

What does God want to accomplish through your writing? Take a moment to really think about it. Beyond your love of writing, beyond your powerful testimony or incredible journey that you want to share, beyond the insight that God has given you in His Word, what role does writing play in the fulfillment of your destiny? In what way is God glorified in and through your writing? Too often we don't think beyond the book or blog post to a greater purpose. But in order to successfully step into the flow, we need to know the reason we write, we need to know our why. And our why, as believers, is rooted not only in what God desires to accomplish in and through our work, but also in and through us that moves beyond the words we pen. Knowing why will help you see yourself and your writing differently.

All that we do, writing included, is rooted in love because everything we do is (or should be) rooted in God, who is love (1 John 4:8). Our love for God should be reflected in a love for His people that reaches beyond the page and lodges in our readers' hearts. So I ask you again: *What does God want to accomplish in and through your writing*? While there will be answers specific to you, to your call, to your experiences and life journey, I believe for all Kingdom writers God desires to communicate His love, to shine His light and to release His life through our work. Knowing purpose, identifying our passions and learning to write in and from love are key to releasing that which impacts lives, transforms us, and honors God.

Write Here, Write Now

Break open your word within me until revelation-light shines out!
Those with open hearts are given insight into your plans.
Psalm 119:130 TPT

God has a plan for you as a writer. In what ways might you express God's light, love, and life in your life, and by extension, through your writing? What do you believe He wants to accomplish through your work?

DEBORAH A. GASTON

For Love of Purpose

> *I admit that I haven't yet acquired the absolute fullness that I'm pursuing, but I run with passion into his abundance so that I may reach the purpose that Jesus Christ has called me to fulfill and wants me to discover.*
> Philippians 3:12 TPT

I've always known I wanted to write, even when I didn't really know that God had a destiny for me or that writing might somehow be a part of that destiny. As I grew in my relationship with the Lord, I became passionate about knowing purpose: my purpose in life, my purpose in ministry, my purpose in writing. The pursuit of purpose gave meaning to my passion for writing. Writing is a means to a greater end. It is a vehicle that aids me in the fulfillment of purpose and destiny.

God has awakened a desire to write in you because it has always been a part of His plan for you. See writing as a gift God has given you that, when used in concert with all your other gifts and talents, helps you walk out destiny and purpose. It is a light He wants you to shine so others see and glorify Him (Matthew 5:16).

Why do you write? What is the message God has given you to share? Do you want to leave a legacy for your family? Do you want to enlighten or educate others? Or do you want to persuade someone to think differently or to take action? Do you want to encourage? Entertain? Knowing your purpose for writing is important to finding your flow and in understanding how God may want to use writing as a part of your destiny. It can also help you make decisions about genre, themes and audience.

Be open as Holy Spirit speaks purpose to you. Each piece of writing will have a specific purpose. So don't box yourself in. You may be comfortable writing nonfiction, but God wants you to share the message He's given you through a fictional piece, a play, or a poem. You may be an incredible storyteller, but God is nudging you to write a memoir. In writing, as in life, purpose is fluid and will change from season to season. Be willing to make the shifts God may call you to make in order to reach those He wants to touch through your work.

Write Here, Write Now

I believe that our destiny and the many purposes for our lives are etched in our DNA, and the gifts and talents we are to use to fulfill purpose are often unveiled in childhood. Those things we are drawn to, those things we give countless hours to, the things we create when left to our own devices, even those things that are play for us may all be key indicators.

Respond to the statement above. What things did you find yourself given over to, finding joy and pleasure in, or play as a child? Can you see them as indicators of purpose and destiny? In what ways? How might your passions be linked to your purpose and destiny?

What role does writing play within your greater purpose and destiny?

The Place of Passion

Purpose is the reason for the journey. Passion is the fire that lights the way.
Author Unknown

There is a rhythm I find when I'm in my writing zone, the place where words ooze from the pen and flow like a stream making its way to something grander, larger, stronger, a river of thought, of stories, of lessons. Their destination beyond my heart, my mind, my hand, beyond the page to a place where they will bring love, light and life. I lose myself in my writing until hours seem like moments. And when I haven't written for long periods of time, I feel it in my soul.

I also have a love for the Word of God and for the people of God. I am passionate about seeing people transformed by God's Word, growing in their relationship with Him, living out purpose. When I am able to marry my love for the Word of God with my love of writing, I feel I am not only living in purpose, but also honoring God who placed both passion and purpose in me. I brim with satisfaction.

Your God-ordained purposes transcend your passions, but your passions may be indicators of purpose. What are you passionate about? You may feel the same way I do about writing. God placed that in you because it is part of His purpose and plan for you. He wants that love to reach through the page and captivate your audience. But you may be someone for whom writing is not necessarily a passion; it has never been something you loved or even desired to do and yet you hear God's call. If a love for writing is not what causes you to pick up the pen or sit for hours before a computer screen, your motivation to write is rooted in something else that you care deeply about. God placed that passion in you and it may be a key to the fulfillment of your destiny. That passion becomes the impetus for your writing. It is important that you identify those passions if you are to find your writing flow.

Passion is defined as "extreme compelling emotion, intense emotional drive or excitement, great anger, rage or fury, enthusiasm or fondness, strong love or affection." Passion is that which excites us, feeds us, motivates us, drives us. Ken Costa writes, "Your passions and dreams are the fuels that feed the fire of God's calling." [8] In other words, our passion often connects us to purpose.

Identifying your passion is important for several reasons. In addition to its connection to purpose, your passion may help determine what you write. If you have a passion for storytelling, there may be a novel gestating inside you. Passion may also help you identify your readers. For example, you may have a heart for children and find you desire to write primarily for them. Keying in on your passion helps you find your writing niche, particularly if that passion has become an area of expertise. It can determine not only *what* you write, but also *how* you write. And, maybe more importantly, if you are writing about something you care deeply about, you will be more motivated to see it to completion.

Your passion(s) may be found in:
- things you enjoy doing
- things that disturb you or even anger you
- things you want to change
- things you lose yourself in for hours
- things you would do, if no one else was impacted or if there was never a paycheck associate with it
- things that bring you a sense of fulfillment

That burning love, that passion in you, is a gift. When linked with purpose, it can empower you to write that novel or collection of poems, to script that play, to pen that memoir, to produce what is in your heart. Share your passion, write your story and change lives!

Write Here, Write Now

We lose ourselves in the things we love. We find ourselves there, too.
Kristin Martz

Make a list of the things you feel passionate about. Choose one and free write about it for 20 minutes. You may tell a story, write a poem or explain why it matters to you. Be creative.

How do you think God will use that passion in your writing?

Nourished and Empowered by Love

> *If you keep my commands, you will live in my love, just as I have kept my Father's commands, for I continually live nourished and empowered by his love.*
> John 15:10 TPT

You are extravagantly loved by the One who has called you to write. Through that love He has gifted you with ideas and words, stories, poems that have the power to communicate His love and impact lives. Kingdom Writer, you have been called to express God's love. That doesn't mean that everything you write speaks directly about the love of God. It does mean that you have been immersed in His love and all you do flows in and from that love.

As you partner with Holy Spirit in the writing process, you are "nourished and empowered" by love in such a way that it pours through you onto the page. Through your authentic voice, your readers sense something different. Often it may be something indefinable, a presence or spirit in the words that causes those who read to feel joy, comfort, a sense of hope, faith, and freedom. It may be something that simply assures them things will get better, releasing life to them.

Write Here, Write Now

Your purpose and passion can fuel you. Think about the book you desire to write. What is the overall purpose for writing it? Who is its intended audience? Narrow the audience—your book is not for everybody. How will you show God's love, light and life through the book? Write an overview of the book.

Writer, Know Thyself

> *If you want to maximize your total potential... you have to know yourself.*
> Mark McGwire

What is important for you as a worshiper who writes is identifying your passion as well as discovering how God chooses to demonstrate His love through you and through your writing. It is important to know who you are, how God has wired you, how He wishes to find expression in you and through you. Often this discovery will lead to a greater understanding of your purpose, the light that shines most brightly through you and through your writing.

What is your grace zone—that place where you feel you are at "home" and everything in you says, "I was born for this"?

Take some time to think about the following questions. Journal what you learn about yourself and how God may wish to find expression in your writing. Remain open, however, to Holy Spirit. He may reveal some things about you that may surprise you and that may shift the direction of your writing.

- Who am I? How do I wish to reveal myself through my work as a writer?
- What experiences have shaped me into the person and the writer I am?
- How do I want to convey my message to the world?
- What perspective do I bring to a subject that may help others see differently?
- What brings life to me and allows my light to shine brightly?
- Where do I find inspiration?
- Am I a storyteller? An encourager? A teacher?
- What kind of books do I prefer to read?
- In what ways does God want me to be fruitful and multiply through my writing?
- How can I use my writing as worship unto God and a gift to others?

You may not be able answer all of these questions now. Use them in your daily journal writing. Listen for the voice of God to speak to you and give you clarity as to the ways He wants to shine through you as a writer.

In the meantime, WRITE! As you do you will discover more about yourself that you can use in your work.

Write Here, Write Now

Man cannot discover new oceans unless he has the courage to lose sight of the shore.
Andre Gide

"Try Something Different" Writing Challenge: Create a poem, a short story, a play on a topic of your choice. Which is most comfortable for you: writing fiction or nonfiction? If fiction is your comfort zone, write a personal essay. If nonfiction is you niche, write a short story or poem. If poetry is easy for you, write in some other form. Step out of your comfort zone. Share the finished product with someone.

Obedience

*If they obey and serve Him,
They shall spend their days in prosperity,
And their years in pleasures.*
Job 36:11

Reflection: A Simple Response

> **Great acts of God are often preceded by simple acts of obedience.**
> Steven Furtick

I was minding my business, going about my merry way, singing a simple song when I heard the whisper. I knew it was God because the idea wasn't remotely anything I had ever considered. It wasn't anything I'd ever dreamed of, prayed for, wished upon on star for. I knew it was God because Deborah wasn't trying to add one more thing to an already jam-packed life, wasn't trying to add a morsel to her already full plate. Knew it was God because not only was this something I had never done before, I had no point of reference for it…at all!

But I'd heard that still small voice. And once you've heard it, you can't un-hear it. You can ignore it. You can choose to disobey it. You can try to flick it away like a fly. But you can't un-hear it.

And I'd heard. So instead of doing what I've done more often than I care to admit, instead of dismissing it as a whim, instead of offering a litany of excuses why I couldn't or why I shouldn't, instead of disqualifying myself, instead of seeking the opinion of those I deemed wiser and more "spiritual," I simply said, "OK."

And that simple response launched me into a new place of fulfillment and solidified purpose beyond anything I had ever dreamed of, prayed for, or wished upon a star for.

The truth is this: Most often, all that is required to hurl us into divine destiny is a simple response. Some of our greatest accomplishments are the result of simply saying, "OK" when God speaks.

He spoke to Noah, "Build an ark." Noah said, "OK," and became the one to repopulate the earth after the flood.

He spoke to Abram, "Leave your country and go to a land I will show you." Abram said, "OK," and became Abraham, the Father of Many Nations, the one through whom all nations would be blessed, the one through whom Messiah came.

He spoke to Moses, "Deliver My people!" Moses said, "OK," and led millions of Israelites out of slavery.

He spoke to a virgin named Mary, "Bear a child!" Mary said, "OK," and gave birth to the Son of God.

He spoke to Peter, "Feed My sheep." Peter said, "OK" and with a simple sermon saw 3000 people saved in one day.

He spoke to Paul, "Preach My Word to the Gentiles." Paul said, "OK" and the gospel was spread, and the Church of Jesus Christ was established all over the then-known world.

He spoke to His Son, "Redeem the world!" Jesus said, "OK," and the Word was made flesh and gave His life to save all mankind.

The greatest adventures in Him, the greatest moments of true ministry, the greatest fulfillment of purpose, the greatest manifestation of His love, light and life through my life have been the result of a simple response when God speaks. Perhaps we have made this life of faith more complicated than it need be. Maybe all it is—all it was ever meant to be—is hearing that still small voice and simply responding, "OK" without needing the details, without putting out fleeces, without getting confirmation from every prophet we know. We simply respond and trust God to confirm His word as we go.

What is God speaking to you? A simple response may not only forever change your life, but the lives of countless others as well.

Write Here, Write Now

...Behold, to obey is better than sacrifice and to heed than the fat of rams.

1 Samuel 15:22b

Write about a time when you obeyed God without question. Be as detailed and creative as possible. What did He instruct you to do? What was the outcome of your obedience? How did you feel when He initially spoke to you? How did you feel afterwards? What did you learn as a result of your obedience?

Obedience: Faith's Fruit

You express love by obedience.
Jack Hyles

Tears pooled in her eyes and she heaved a sigh. "I really believe God wants me to write my testimony. He has been so good, and He has delivered and healed me of so much. But, not only is it hard to re-tell, I don't want people to know the person I was. I'd rather them just know me as I am now."

"Let me ask this," I whispered. "What matters more: protecting your image or obeying God?"

If we shift our perspective to see writing as an act of worship, we must see obedience as a key component. We have defined a worshiper as one who is intimately acquainted with and one who has a daily relationship with God exhibited through obedience, and we have talked about the role of faith in the writing process. Obedience is inextricably connected to faith. Nineteenth century poet, Christina Rossetti, wrote: "Obedience is the fruit of faith." God speaks to our hearts, "Create! Write! Produce!" Our faith in what He says calls us to respond. We obediently create, write, produce.

Obedience begins by simply saying, "Yes." Our "yes" to Holy Spirit more perfectly aligns us with God's purposes and plans for us. Our "yes" releases grace that empowers us to do all that is necessary to fulfill the call. And our "yes" postures us to receive all that is available to us—both spiritually and naturally—to walk through the process to its end. We find peace and satisfaction in obedience because it is through obedience that we become who God always intended…

We become the writers He is calling us to be.

Settle It and Write

Delight yourself also in the Lord,
And He shall give you the desires of your heart.
Psalm 37:4

Is this really God or is it just me? As worshipers we want nothing more than to obey God and to know we are in His will. We feel a prompting in our hearts to write, but we often question whether that is something God is prompting us to do or if it's just something we'd like to do. We look for confirmation, but there is no burning bush, no flash of lightning, no James-Earl-Jones voice booming from heaven. We let our fear of being wrong, our fear of missing God stop us from taking any action at all. Or we relegate our writing to journals that no one else will ever read.

I am convinced that the very desire—especially if it persists—is confirmation enough. The psalmist instructs us in Psalm 37:4 to delight in the Lord with the promise that He will give us the desires of our hearts. The Hebrew word translated "delight" literally means to be pliable. When you and I are pliable before the Lord, when we delight in Him, He places desires in our hearts. His desires become our desires; we want what He wants for us. He so naturally places those stirrings in our hearts that we may not realize they are from Him. God has placed the desire to write in you because, through you, He desires to change lives, heal souls, advance His Kingdom. He has placed the desire there so His glory may be manifested in and through your work. Your book is a love song to Him. He has placed the desire in your heart because it's the song He now longs to hear!

Fear is often the reason we don't fully obey when we sense the call to write. Most of us would like to believe that, no matter how challenging or great the sacrifice, we will obey the Lord when He speaks. But it's so easy to disregard or dismiss the nudging of Holy Spirit in the simple things like writing. It becomes easy to convince ourselves that our writing is a small thing. And yet, our yes, our obedience in both the great and the small pleases God.

Settle it. God is stirring you. Say yes and write.

Yes to the Lord, Yes to the Work

The creative process is a process of surrender, not control.
Julia Cameron

We find our flow in the place of surrender. Once we are able to surrender much, of the struggle ceases, and we are ushered into a place of grace. Surrendering to God is a source of power, for all our creativity flows from Him. And just as we surrender to the Lord, we must learn to surrender to the work itself.

Madeleine L'Engle, author of *A Wrinkle in Time*, spoke of this kind of obe-dience in her book about faith and art, *Walking on Water*. She suggests that we must be obedient to the work, explaining that each work—no matter how great or seemingly insignificant—whispers to us, "Give me life." We have a choice. We can say no to the work and not write at all. Or we fail to listen to the work itself and produce something far less than God desires and deserves; we produce inferior work. L'Engle believed that is saying no also. When we listen and obey, when we are willing to serve the work, we produce something far beyond our natural abilities. She writes:

> When the artist is truly the servant of the work, the work is better than the artist; Shakespeare knew how to listen to his work, and so he often wrote better than he could; Bach composed more deeply, more truly, than he knew; Rembrandt's brush put more of the human spirit on canvas than Rembrandt could comprehend.[9]

When you simply say yes to God and begin, you will find that the work itself will direct you. Yes, you begin with a plan, an outline, a destination, but as you listen and write, as you allow the work to speak, you will find new paths, possibly even a new destination. Obedience to both the call and to the work can lead you into new realms of creativity.

Write Here, Write Now

> **Obedience is less painful than regret.**
> Christine Caine

Take a moment and listen. What work is calling to you? How will you respond? What might be the consequences of not saying yes?

Believe in this moment that both God and the work are waiting, listening for your response. Your obedience in this moment can shift your life and the lives of others who are waiting for what only you can produce. Write your response.

Commitment, Not Convenience

> *Commit your way to the* Lord,
> *Trust also in Him,*
> *And He shall bring it to pass.*
> Psalm 37:5

> **Without commitment, nothing happens.**
> T.D. Jakes

I am intrigued with those who find great success in life, whether authors or athletes, educators or entrepreneurs. Whether they were born privileged or grew up with nothing but a dream, they all have something in common. It's not that they are extremely gifted, highly intelligent, well-educated or even highly motivated. It's not that they had family who supported their dreams and encouraged them. What makes the difference in their lives is their level of commitment to seeing the dream become a reality. Those who find success commit and discipline themselves to do what is necessary to accomplish their goals.

So many things vie for our time. Career, ministry, family, and a host of other responsibilities can, if we allow them, squeeze writing out of the mix. We say, "I'll get to it." Sometimes we do; most times we don't. We allow everything and everyone else to take precedence in our lives and the books yearning to be birthed remain in that embryonic state. But when we understand that God has placed in us the desire to write, see it as our offering of worship, and understand that obedience is key in establishing the writing life we desire, we become intentional about knocking down every excuse and making a commitment to do the work.

The simple truth is this: if we are to respond obediently to the call to write, writing cannot be a matter of convenience. We don't wait until we *feel* inspired. We have to be willing to commit by ordering our days and our time to do the work.

Let me say this before going any further: this is not to guilt you into writing. Guilt is no motivation. You have to decide the place writing has (or you desire it to have) in your life in this season. You have to decide if it is something you really are willing to commit to. You have to decide if this is the right time for you, and if it's not, that is perfectly OK. No guilt. No condemnation. As Solomon said, there is a time for everything.

But you also have to be sure that the reasons you offer for not writing—especially if you believe you are called to write and really have the desire—are not rooted in something else. Is it really that you are just too busy and don't have the time or is it perfectionism, feelings of inadequacy, comparison? These are not reasons. These are enemies birthed from fear that are only conquered by writing.

If, however, you are ready to commit (and if you are still reading, I believe you are ready) remember that obedience requires intentionality! Our yes to God cannot be in word only; our yes must be followed by action. In order to give birth to the book that is incubating in you, you must develop a greater writing discipline and establish a plan that works for you—one that will be easy for you to stick with so you finish what you begin.

A Goal and a Plan

The goal without a plan is just a wish.
Antoine de Saint-Exupery

If we are to respond to the call of God to write, we must set goals and develop a plan for achieving them. This, too, is an act of faith. It says, "Lord, I believe that You have chosen me to share my story with others. I will now align myself with Your word by doing that which is necessary to complete the work You've given me."

Now is the time to make decisions that will move you towards your writing goals. Where and when will you write? How often will you write? Are you a morning person or is night your peak time? Many writers prefer mornings because the mind is clear and the heart is open. However, mornings don't work for everyone. You know the flow of your day. Determine what works best for you. You may look at your day and think you cannot squeeze one more thing in, but we find time for that which is important to us. Is writing a priority? Then you will find the time, even if it means getting up bit earlier in the morning or staying up a bit later at night. Set a time and make it sacred. Build it into your schedule, place it on your calendar, set reminders on your phone.

Begin small, if necessary. The amount of time you carve out or how much you write during that time is not as important as being consistent. Some days you may only be able to get one sentence on the page. Write that one sentence. Make it the best sentence you can. Relish it. Thank God for it. Then walk away and return to it the next day. Holy Spirit and that sentence will be waiting for you with open arms.

Create the space for writing. I don't know about you, but there are certain environments that I find more conducive for writing than others. It's important to create a writing space that will inspire you to write. That space should be free of clutter, and have readily available all you need—computer, pens, paper, reference books, etc. Surround yourself with things that spawn creativity.

If home doesn't work for you, find a spot that does. Sometimes a simple change of scenery can boost creativity. You may even want to consider a personal writing retreat. Some of my most productive times have been when I've been able to get away for two or three days. If you are serious about writing, you find the time and the place.

Minimize distractions. You don't have to check every text message, respond to every email, answer every call. Decide that during your writing time you will place the phone on silent, close all tabs on your browser and write! Let people in your life know that this is your regular time to write and you will get back with them later. If it's not an emergency, it can wait. Your writing time is time with the Lord.

You can fulfill your writing dream! Commit your way to God, trust Him and see what He does when you do your part.

Write Here, Write Now

Commitment is what transforms a promise into a reality.
Abraham Lincoln

Read Psalm 37:4-5. What do these verses say to you as it relates to your commitment to write?

Take a moment to survey your days and weeks. Where can you find blocks of time you can devote to writing? Remember these don't have to be large chunks of time—10 minutes of writing is better than none. How many days can you commit to? Block out the days and times you will write on your calendar.

Now think of places that are conducive for writing. Is there a space in your home that you can dedicate as your writing spot? What do you need to make that space special and inviting? What is needed so the space says, "A writer works here"?

Write a writer's manifesto and place it where you can see it to remind yourself of your commitment to write.

Finding Your Voice

Finding your voice is a process, a journey to the center of you.
April Erwin

What can I say that hasn't already been said? How can I be original in my writing? These are questions novice writers often ask. Perhaps, however, the goal is not finding new themes to write about. Perhaps the goal is not originality, but authenticity and learning to bring our unique perspective to age-old themes. Canadian author, Charles de Lint, wrote, "Don't forget—no one else sees the world the way you do, so no one else can tell the stories that you have to tell." Not only can no one tell the stories you can, no one can tell them the way you can. What you bring to a subject is your own unique perspective expressed in your unique voice. We must strive to develop a writing voice that enables us to communicate our perspective and allows our audience to know us through our writing.

An Act of Discovery

Your writing voice is simply the way you sound on paper. It is your personality, style, sense of humor, life experiences revealed in how you use language. Your writing voice distinguishes you from other writers. Because people connect to people, your voice draws readers to the person revealed through the words, causing them to want to read your work. It is found in word choice; it is found in the cadence of your words; it is found in the structure of your sentences. It signals to your reader that you have settled into your identity as a writer and allows them to know you through your work.

When I told my father I wanted to write, and he gave me this advice: "Read, read, read. Find authors you really like and emulate their style until you develop your own voice." You see, all of us are influenced by others and we most often learn by imitation. We often draw from those whose works we read, either consciously or unconsciously. But as we infuse our personality, our life experiences, our soul into our writing, something authentic and powerful emerges—something that is uniquely ours. We find our own voice.

It takes courage and time, but it makes such a difference in our ability to connect with our readers.

How do you find your authentic voice? There is no easy way, no "30 Days to Finding Your Voice" guide available that I know of. It will take time to discover who you are as a writer and develop your voice, but here are a few tips that will help:
- Read, read, read, and read some more. Learn to read like a writer. That means you are not just reading for information or enjoyment. You are paying attention to how authors use language, create pictures, structure sentences. What can you learn about the writer by the word choices he or she makes? What distinguishes him or her from other writers?
- Write, write, write, and write some more. Author Stephen King said, "If you want to be a writer, you must do two things above all others: read a lot and write a lot. There's no way around these two things that I'm aware of, no shortcut."[10] The more you write and experiment with language, the more of your writer self you will discover.
- Read your writing aloud. Do you have a rhythm? Does your writing create images in your mind? Does it evoke certain emotions? Are you conversational, scholarly, humorous? Is your language sophisticated, flowery, lyrical, or straight to the point?
- Experiment with different styles of writing and different genres.
- Don't be afraid to be vulnerable. Don't be afraid to take risks.
- Glean from other writers. Authenticity is found when we meld what we've gained from others with our own sense of self.

Echoing the Voice of God

I believe there is another aspect to finding our voice that we cannot overlook as Kingdom writers—discovering the voice of God within our voice. We cannot overlook whose voice we are called to echo in the world. No matter what genre, as worshipers called to write, He has called us by His grace to communicate His heart, to be His voice. Listen. How does He speak to you? How does He speak through you? What is the sound of His voice within your spirit? How can you reflect His Voice in the words you write, in your style, in your tone?

When we read the Scriptures, it is clear that the Apostle Paul's voice is distinct from Peter's or John's. David's authentic voice in the psalms is not the same as other psalmists. While each person was inspired by Holy Spirit, each person's experience, perspective, personality, purpose in writing and use of language are unique. Each echo God's voice in a signature, authentic way.

And so it is with us. Though the heart of our message is inspired by Holy Spirit, we remain keenly aware that He uses our voice, our personality, our words, our creativity. It is a melding of the divine and the human. God pours ideas and concepts into us, and yet allows us the freedom to choose and craft them in a way that helps others hear His heart within our voice, in our words. That is the beauty and joy of co-authoring with Him. The voices become one and ring distinctly on every page.

Silent No More
God has given you a message and He has given you a voice! There is nothing more that the enemy would love to do than silence your voice and silence the voice of God in you. God's words flowing from your pen are powerful. God's desire is that through writing you discover your authentic voice and carry the message that He has given you to those who are waiting. You can no longer be silent! Be courageous! Find your voice and write the truth that has the ability to set others free!

We return to the importance of knowing yourself, not just the writer, but as the unique and beautiful individual God created you to be. And that is an ongoing process. The person you are today is not the person you were last year or will be in ten years. You are becoming who God has always intended you to be, and that person will shine through your authentic voice.

Write Here, Write Now

Find your voice and inspire others to find theirs.
Stephen Covey

Think of an event from your life that has some emotion, suspense, humor, or through which you learned a profound lesson that Holy Spirit used to change or mature you. Make sure it involves at least one other person and that you are the main character. Write two versions of the story. One that is just a straightforward telling of the event from your point of view. Then write another version either from the point of view of the other person involved (still in first person) or from the third-person point of view (someone outside the story looking down on the action and narrating).

Read aloud something you have written. What do you notice about your voice, your writing style? Does it sound generic, as if anyone could have written it or does it reflect your personality? In what ways? Rewrite it to capture more of your personality, your authentic voice.

Worship

Surely, no matter what you are doing (speaking, writing, or working), do it all in the name of Jesus our Master, sending thanks through Him to God our Father.

Colossians 3:17 The VOICE

Reflection: The Glory's in the Finish

Beginning in itself has no value, it is an end which makes beginning meaningful; we must end what we began.
Amit Kalantri

As I look back over my life, I realize that there have been lots of "start-to-stop-to-start-all-over-again" moments, and even more "start-to-stop-to-never-start-again" moments. I will never know the measure and degree of blessings I've missed because of my failure to finish some of the things I began. May never know how God desired to reveal His glory in and through those things. I have learned over the years that the greatest manifestation of God's glory in our lives isn't in beginning, but in finishing what we've begun. After all, who ever heard, "All's well that *begins* well"?

That's because the glory is in the finished work.

We see this truth throughout scripture. In Exodus 25, God speaks to Moses, "Let them make Me a sanctuary that I may dwell among them." Then in the forty days that Moses spent in the presence of God on the mountain, he received detailed instructions for building the tabernacle. As we read through the remaining chapters of Exodus, we see this phrase repeated: *"And Moses did, according to all that the Lord had commanded him, so he did."*

The Lord spoke and, by faith, Moses responded to the word of the Lord through obedience.

Then we read this simple yet profound statement in Exodus 40:33b. "*. . . and Moses finished the work.*" He left nothing undone! He didn't skip a step! He didn't devise a shortcut. He didn't start and then decide there were more pressing things to do (after all, leading a stiff-necked people is a full-time job). He didn't decide that it was enough to have the Ark of the Covenant and neglect everything else God had instructed. He didn't allow the magnitude of the task to halt him. He didn't allow resistance and distractions to derail him. He didn't allow weariness to cause him to cease. He finished the work!

What follows astonishes me every time I read it: *"Then the cloud covered the tabernacle of meeting and the glory of the Lord filled the tabernacle. And Moses was not able to enter the tabernacle of meeting, because the cloud rested above it, and the glory of the Lord filled the tabernacle"* (Exodus 40:34,35).

There is a progression here that we can easily miss. The Lord spoke. Moses obeyed. Moses finished the work. *Then* the glory of the Lord filled the house. We see that same progression in the life and ministry of Jesus Christ. He prayed in John 17:4,5: "I have glorified You on earth. I have *finished* the work which You have given Me to do. And now, O Father, *glorify* Me together with Yourself, with the glory I had with You before the world was" (emphasis added).

Through His obedience to His Father, Jesus finished the work He was sent to do, and the glory of God was manifested in Him for all to see!

It has taken me a long time to birth *Finding Your F.L.O.W.*, and as I draw closer to its completion, I have a peace and I'm filled with a sense of satisfaction. I have completed the work that God has given me. Where it goes or how it impacts Kingdom writers is out of my hands. It is all in God's hands now! I choose to believe His glory rests on this finished work and that I am better for having completed what I began.

May it be so with you! Be resolute! God has given you a work to do. Commit to finish because…

The glory is in the finish!

Write Here, Write Now

I have glorified you on the earth by completing down to the last detail what you assigned me to do.
John 17:4 The Message

Write about a time you began something but did not complete it. What kept you from completing the work? How did not completing it make you feel? Is this something you can complete now or is it too late? What do you think you may have missed by not completing the task?

What writing project have you begun but not yet completed? Where are you in the process? What will you need to do to complete the work?

Devise a plan to get it done within the next 90 days. Break it down into small stages. What can you do each day that moves you closer to completion? Then share the plan with someone who will lovingly hold you accountable. Set a deadline for the completion of each task.

DEBORAH A. GASTON

The Worshipful Work of Writing

> *So here's what I want you to do, God helping you: Take your everyday, ordinary life—your sleeping, eating, going-to-work, and walking-around life—and place it before God as an offering. Embracing what God does for you is the best thing you can do for him.*
> Romans 12:1 The Message

Novelist and essayist, Thomas Mann wrote, "A writer is someone for whom writing is more difficult than it is for other people." Our readers never fully understand the labor behind the words we present to them. There are days when the words flow like water, but there are days when we agonize to produce one coherent sentence. We can spend an hour in search of just the right word, or write page after page after page, only to delete most of it because it just doesn't work. But as we see writing as an offering to the Lord, we learn to relish the work. As Kingdom writers, we want to present to God the best that's in us. We also want to offer our audience that which represents Him well. And that takes time and hard work.

It doesn't matter how gifted, talented or creative you are. It doesn't matter if you are a grammar wiz or master wordsmith. Writing is work! It takes time and effort to write a book, article, blog post that draws your readers in, holds their attention, and concisely captures all you wish to convey. We must approach writing as work, knowing that our work, too, is worship. In fact, one of the Hebrew words used in the Bible for working in one's calling is the same word used for worshiping. If writing is your calling, then the work necessary to fulfill that calling is as much an offering of worship as the finished product. Keeping that in mind will make it easier to remain focused and to push through any frustration when the work gets challenging.

Writing is a process. The stages of the writing process may overlap at times, but each one is necessary to produce a work of excellence. And, as with any process, it takes time and resolve. To skip any of the stages or try to shortcut your way around any of them can result in creating more work in the long run or in producing an inferior work. Embracing each stage of the process is key in finding your writing flow.

The stages of the writing process include prewriting, drafting, revising, and editing. The prewriting stage, the stage where we pray, we research, we brainstorm, we journal, we read, is essential. This is where we take a concept, narrow it down to something workable, gain all the knowledge we can and develop a plan. Every writer must begin with a plan—a map or outline. That plan may alter as you write. That's the nature of writing when you allow Holy Spirit to guide you. But you don't want to begin without some idea of where you're headed, what you want your readers to gain by the end of the journey and how you will guide them there.

Once you have prayed and have a plan, begin your first draft. Write with the understanding that it is just that—*a first draft*. Your main focus is getting the ideas down. British author Terry Pratchett said, "The first draft is just you telling yourself the story." You're not concerned with all the technical aspects of writing such as grammar and punctuation. That will happen later in the process. Begin by following your outline and just writing! Let go of perfectionism and just write. This is often the most difficult thing for novice writers (and recovering perfectionists like me). No writer gets it all right when writing the first draft (and often when writing the second and third drafts). You want to get your ideas out and on to the page. Resist the temptation to edit as you go. It will slow you down. Just write. Be OK with some bad writing initially. That, too, is part of the process.

During the drafting stage, you want to write from your heart more than from your head. While you have an outline or map, don't focus so much on the outline that you aren't listening to Holy Spirit. There is a spiritual dynamic at work that leads the Kingdom writer to places of discovery, insight, revelation. Allow Holy Spirit to guide you through those places even if it is a departure from your outline.

Don't grow too attached to the first draft. Your writing will change multiple times before you have that finished piece. Much of the real work comes in revising and editing. You must be willing to rewrite, revise and edit as many times as necessary until you have the best piece of writing possible (Ernest Hemingway rewrote *A Farewell to Arms* 50 times). Newberry Medal winner,

Rebecca Stead gives this insight: "The writing process is not just putting down one page after another—it's a lot of writing and then rewriting, restructuring the story, changing the way things come together." It's not about perfection, but it is about excellence. Be willing to revise and reshape it to create a work of excellence.

It will all come together as it should in God's perfect timing as you lend yourself to the work. More is being accomplished than you realize as you work towards a finished, polished piece. You are being transformed in the process! Trust Holy Spirit. Surrender to the work. Embrace the process and enjoy the journey.

Write Here, Write Now

> *I want to suggest that you finish what you started to do a year ago... Having started the ball rolling so enthusiastically, you should carry this project through to completion just as gladly, giving whatever you can out of whatever you have. Let your enthusiastic idea at the start be equalled by your realistic action now.*
>
> 2 Corinthians 8:10-11 TLB

Where are you in the writing process? Do you still have an idea that needs to be developed? Have you started the first draft and still need to complete it or and are you ready to rewrite and edit?

If you have not begun, sit quietly. Pray and ask Holy Spirit to direct you through the prewriting stage. What topic or idea is speaking to you? Write the topic at the of a page in your journal. Then free write everything you currently know or want to know about that topic. Read over what you have written. What do you need to research? Which ideas will you use? Create an outline for your book.

If you have a completed draft, take some time to read what you have written so far. Does it have a flow? Does it reflect your authentic voice? Does it say what you want to say in a way that is clear to your intended audience? Make notes of changes you want to make.

The Worship of Our Words

...The words I speak are spirit, and they are life.
John 6:63b

A writer is a person who cares what words mean, what they say, how they say it. Writers know words are their way towards truth and freedom, and so they use them with care, with thought, with fear, with delight.
Ursula L. LeGuin

One of my favorite passages of scripture is John 1, which speaks of Jesus as the Word—the Logos. The Greek word *logos* simply means "the expression of thought." [11] Jesus is the expression of God's thoughts! He is the Living Word! And His very life not only reveals who God is but also God's thoughts concerning you and me.

The Hebrews have an interesting concept of words that I believe will help us as Kingdom writers. Words are more than units for communication; they are a manifestation of the substance of the person speaking them. Simply put, the words we use reveal or reflect who we are. Just as The Word (Logos) was a revelation of the heart, mind and character of God, our words—written or spoken—reveal our heart, mind and character.

As image bearers, our words are not only representative of who we are, but also of the One who called us to write. Our words should reflect the love, life and light of Christ. We have power to inspire, to encourage, to heal through the words we choose, but we also have the ability to produce the opposite if we are not careful. We are accountable for our words! We must understand this as we write and be intentional when choosing them.

I have a love for words! They dance before me, within me, inviting me to dance with them and create a ballet of words choreographed by love. I collect them like precious gems. I have come to appreciate them as gifts. In his book *Learning to Speak God from Scratch*, Jonathan Merritt writes, "Words are one of God's holy gifts to humanity and speaking them should be a sacred act."[12] I believe not only should we speak them as a sacred act, we should write them as a sacred act. There is life in the words we use. As Kingdom writers, we have a responsibility to choose and use them wisely and thoughtfully.

In the practical sense, broadening our vocabulary will enhance our writing. Words paint pictures, create images, express and evoke emotion, create constructs. Just any word will not do. We must be intentional while being mindful that in writing "less is more." We want our audience to grow, but we must speak to them in terms they understand. Good writers learn to express ideas in the fewest words. Choose words that are precise and concise. Your goal is not to impress your audience with your extensive vocabulary. Your goal is to inspire, enlighten, encourage, entertain, speak truth in a way your readers connect with, and that elevates them at the same time.

The dictionary and thesaurus can be invaluable. But one of the best ways to enhance your vocabulary is by reading. In his book *On Writing*, Stephen King writes: "If you don't have time to read, you don't have the time or the tools to write."[10] Reading not only helps to build your vocabulary, but it helps you see how to craft words into powerful sentences. Writers learn by reading how to use (or not use) words.

Remember words are a gift from God! Grow to appreciate the value of this gift and use words in ways that enable your readers to think on things that are "authentic and real, honorable and admirable, beautiful and respectful, pure and holy, merciful and kind" (Philippians 4:8a TPT).

Write Here, Write Now

> *Have something to say, and say it as clearly as you can.*
> *That is the only secret of style.*
> Matthew Arnold

Choose a piece you have written. Read it aloud (or have someone read it to you). What do you hear as you read? Does it sound lyrical? Does it sound flat? Does it sound repetitious? Have you used concrete nouns and verbs? Or are you using a lot of modifiers instead (adjectives or adverbs where one precise noun or verb will do)? Do many of your sentences begin the same way (with an -ing word or a phrase beginning with the word "as")? Have you used a lot of unnecessary words?

Read something from one of your favorite authors. What about his or her writing appeals to you? What can you glean from this piece of writing that you can apply to your own?

Rewrite your piece using concrete, precise and specific words that paint an image in the reader's mind.

Worth It All

> *...that you may walk worthy of the Lord, fully pleasing Him, being fruitful in every good work and increasing in the knowledge of God...*
> Colossians 1:10

Kingdom Writer, understand that your worth is not found in the number of book sales, the number of blog followers or the number of likes you receive on social media. There is nothing wrong with those things, and I pray your book sales soar and doors of opportunity open for you as a result of completing and publishing your book. But neither your worth nor the true worth of the work lie in those things. Your worth rests in the One who created you. What you have been called to do as a writer has worth as you embrace the work God has given you, as you obey His voice throughout the writing process and trust Him with the results.

One of the definitions of "worth" found in *The Webster's New World Dictionary* is "the quality of a person or thing that lends importance, value, merit, etc. and that is measurable by the esteem in which the person or thing is held." Knowing that God highly esteems you is what matters most. Then whatever flows from you that is in alignment with His call on your life has worth as well.

Is it worth the hard work, the time and sacrifice, the money, the challenges we often face as writers? Is it worth it, even if you don't sell hundreds or thousands of books? Is it worth it if some readers don't quite get you?

Yes! Knowing you have been obedient to the call makes it worth it. Offering God worship from the substance your being makes it worth it. The transformation and growth you experience while walking through the process makes it worth it. Maximizing the gifts and talents God has blessed you with makes it worth it! Seeing even one life impacted by what you've penned makes it worth it. Walking in purpose and fulfilling destiny makes it worth it. Becoming a little bit more of who God created you to be makes it worth it. Honoring God in the ways that make Him smile makes it worth it!

As you see worship in a different context, you will see your life and all you give yourself to as your love song to God. Your writing is produced out of your substance as a gift to Him. When, by faith, you simply respond to the call to create, He delights in ways you cannot fathom.

Your authentic worship is found in using what He has given you for His glory. He has given you creative ideas for books, articles, blogs and so much more. Breathe life into that which has yet to come alive! Produce fruit that remains and touches the hearts of future generations.

You are called to create! You are called to write! Write, knowing that through each word God gets the glory!

My prayer for you is that you walk worthy of the call to write, pleasing God through faith, love, obedience and worship. May you enter into this wonderful creative space with Him and be fruitful in every good work. May you be His poetry, showing forth His glory through that which you create. May you always *FLOW*.

Putting It All Together

We have become his poetry, a re-created people that will fulfill the destiny he has given each of us, for we are joined to Jesus, the Anointed One. Even before we were born, God planned in advance our destiny and the good works we would do to fulfill it!"
Ephesians 2:10 TPT

[Writing] is a matter of persistence and faith and hard work. So you might as well go ahead and get started.
Anne Lamott

Let's sum it all up now with keys to finding your flow. It is time to step fully into the space God has called you to as a Kingdom Writer.

- Pray (you may use the prayer at the beginning of this book if you wish). Be still. Listen. Holy Spirit is your creative partner in the writing process. Allow Him to guide you.
- See writing as your authentic expression of worship, pleasing to God.
- Just Write. Write when you're inspired; write when you're not inspired. Write when you feel like it; write when you don't feel like it. You don't become a great writer by talking about writing, by reading books about writing, or thinking about writing, but by writing.
- Allow your faith to override all fear and doubt.
- Recognize the voice of your inner critics and silence them. Replace the lies they whisper with the truth of God's Word. Remind yourself that you are a writer and that you have something worth saying.
- Know yourself.
- Find *your* voice and tell *your* story. Be courageous enough to write about your fears, failures, successes, dreams, insecurities—all the things that make you human and relatable. Don't hide.
- Don't compare yourself to other writers. God fashioned you just the way He wanted you to be so He could shine through you in a unique way. Be who He created you to be.

- Know your purpose—know your why. Ask God what He has called you to do. Ask Him how writing connects with your greater purpose and destiny.
- Know your audience. Your work is not for everyone—not even all Christians.
- Read! Read! Read! Don't limit yourself to your favorite writers or favorite genres. There is something to be gleaned from good writers.
- Realize that in Christ you have been made free. Write from that place of freedom. Don't limit yourself. Be led by Holy Spirit.
- Develop and maintain your own writing routine. Realize that what works for other writers may not work for you. Find what works for you and then work it.
- Be intentional. Make writing a priority.
- Don't strive for perfection; strive for excellence.
- Invest in yourself as a writer. Take a class, join a writer's group, attend a conference or go on a writer's retreat.
- Stretch yourself, but don't stress yourself.
- Find an accountability partner.
- Stay rooted in faith, love, obedience and worship.

Afterthoughts

*And we know that God causes all things to work together
for good to those who love God, to those who are called
according to His purpose.*
Romans 8:28 NASB

The book you are reading is the result of a simple response to the voice of God. It is not the book I wanted to write. It is, however, the book I *needed* to write. Not because the world needs another book on writing. Just go to Amazon and search. There is no dearth of books by writers telling other writers how to write. Not because Christian writers have a need for a book like this. Not because I believe God has given me a unique perspective as a worshiper who writes. And not because it could (and I pray it does) benefit other worshipers who write.

My need to write this book transcends the book itself. As I was writing (and wrestling) with *F.LO.W.*, Holy Spirit reminded me of something He'd spoken to me nearly two decades ago: "Your life is the lesson. Track the process." That is when I understood the writing of this book was not just about writing a book. I cannot write that which I have not lived and embodied. I needed to walk through the process, beyond the stages from prewriting to publication, to learn more about myself and about the God who called me. I needed to be drawn deeper into the *FLOW*, both as a worshiper and a writer. God took a simple concept—writing as worship—and turned it into a deeply personal life lesson that has been transformative.

I have always endeavored to live a life of faith, love, obedience and worship, but God has used this book to bring me to a greater level of faith, greater depths of love, a deeper commitment to absolute obedience, and deeper levels of intimate worship. I have been brought to places of repentance as I have had to realign my thinking with *all* God says about me. I have found freedom by confronting my fears, exposing the lies, staring down the enemies that sought to silence me, sought to pull me away from purpose, or simply to wear me down so I'd just give up. I have learned the power of perseverance. I have learned to rely completely on and rest securely in His immeasurable grace that enables and empowers me to be the writer and the worshiper He created me to be. More importantly, I have seen God in new ways as He drew me deeper into the *F.L.O.W.*

All from writing a book. For the Kingdom writer there is always more that God wants to accomplish *in* us than *through* our work. When we sit to pen the book longing to be written, we embark on a journey to the interior. We emerge healed, we emerge stronger, we emerge changed. We become the message of the book and the words we pen have greater impact for they reflect a life that has been transformed by God. The words have deeper meaning as a result.

I pray that you have seen yourself in *Finding Your F.L.O.W.*, that it mirrors, to some degree, your writing journey, and it has inspired and encouraged you to simply say yes to the call and to become the message. As you live in and from the *FLOW*, as you remain rooted in faith, love, obedience and worship, more is accomplished in you and through your writing than you can imagine.

Live in and from the *FLOW*. Find your voice and refuse to be silent.

Live in and from the *FLOW*. Find the strength, confidence and grace to be the writing worshiper you were created to be.

Live in and from the *FLOW*. Find the freedom to speak truth that brings freedom to others.

Live in and from the *FLOW*. Find the place where passion and purpose intersect and find fulfillment.

Live in and from the *FLOW*. See God's glory manifest as you use all you are and all you have as worship unto Him.

Endnotes

1. Stevenson, John W. *Worshiper by Design: A Unique Look at Why We Were Created* (Kindle Location 217-220). BookBaby. Kindle Edition.

2. Ibid (Kindle Location 222-223). Bookbaby. Kindle Edition.

3. Stream of Consciousness is a literary device of narration that describes in words the flow of thoughts in the mind of the characters.

4. Purcell, M. (2016). "The Health Benefits of Journaling". Psych Central. https://psychcentral.com/lib/the-health-benefits-of-journaling/

5. Toit, Francois Du (2014-01-08). *Mirror Bible: A Selection of Key New Testament Texts Paraphrased from the Greek* (Kindle Locations 25446-25448). Mirror Word Publishing (Kindle Edition by Ten 10 Ebooks).

6. Pressfield, Steven. *The War of Art* (p 40). Black Irish Entertainment LLC. Kindle Edition.

7. Simmons, Brian. *Romans: Grace and Glory*, The Passion Translation. Broadstreet. 2014.

8. Costa, Ken. *Know Your Why: Finding and Fulfilling Your Calling in Life* (p. 4) Thomas Nelson. Kindle Edition.

9. L'Engle, Madeleine. *Walking on Water: Reflections on Faith and Art*. WaterBrook Press. 1972, p. 17.

10. King, Stephen. *On Writing: A Memoir on the Craft*. Scribner. 2000, p. 145.

11. *The New Strong's Expanded Dictionary of Bible Words* explains that *logos* (#3056) denotes the expression of thought as the embodiment of a concept or idea.

12. Merritt, Jonathan. *Learning God from Scratch* (p. 45). The Crown Publishing Group. Kindle Edition.

Bibliography

Blatchford, Faith. *Creativity Soza: Unlocked Inspiration, Imagination, Innovation.* Age to Come Publishing, 2014.

Brogan, Chris. *Finding Your Writing Voice.* Kindle Edition, 2016.

Cameron, Julia. *The Artist's Way: A Spiritual Path to Higher Creativity.* New York: Jeremy P. Tarcher/Putnam, 2002.

Costa, Ken. *Know Your Why: Finding and Fulfilling Your Calling in Life.* Nashville: W Publishing, 2016.

DuToit, Francois. *Mirror Study Bible: The Romance of the Ages.* Mirror Word Publishing, 2012

Elsheimer, Janice. *The Creative Call: An Artist's Response to the Way of the Spirit.* Waterbridge Press, 2001.

Goldberg, Natalie. *Writing Down the Bones: Freeing the Writer Within.* Boston: Shambala, 2005.

King, Stephen. *On Writing: A Memoir on the Craft.* New York: Scribner, 2000.

LaMott, Anne. *Bird by Bird: Some Instructions on Writing and Life.* New York: Anchor Books, 2005.

L' Engle, Madeleine. *Walking on Water: Reflections on Faith and Art.* Waterbrook Press, 1972.

Levoy, Gregg. *Callings: Finding and Following an Authentic Life.* New York: Three Rivers Press, 1997.

Lizorkin-Eyzenberg, Eli. *Jewish Insights into Scripture.* Kindle Edition, 2019.

McManus, Erwin Raphael. *The Artisan Soul: Crafting Your Life as a Work of Art.* HarperOne, 2015.

Merritt, Jonathan. *Learning God from Scratch: Why Sacred Words are Vanishing and How We Can Revive Them.* New York: The Crown Publishing Group, 2018.

Mounce, William D. *Mounce's Complete Expository of Old and New Testament Words.* Zondervan, 2006.

Pressfield, Steven. *The War of Art: Break through the Blocks and Win Your Creative Battles.* Black Irish Entertainment LLC. Kindle Edition, 2019.

Schaeffer, Franky. *Addicted to Mediocrity: 20th Century Christians and the Arts.* Westchester: Crossway Books, 1981.

Simmons, Brian. *Romans: Grace and Glory*, The Passion Translation. Racine, Wisconsin: Broadstreet Publishing, 2014.

Stevenson, John W. *Worshiper by Design: A Unique Look at Why We Were Created.* Xulon Press, 2009.

Strong, James. *The Strong's Expanded Dictionary of Bible Words.* Nashville: Thomas Nelson Publishers, 2001.

www.ingramcontent.com/pod-product-compliance
Lightning Source LLC
Chambersburg PA
CBHW071359080526
44587CB00017B/3134